HAUNTED
NORTH
CENTRAL TEXAS

HAUNTED
NORTH
CENTRAL TEXAS

TERESA NORDHEIM

Haunted
America

Published by Haunted America
A Division of The History Press
Charleston, SC
www.historypress.com

Front cover: QuesterMark.
Back cover, top: Lewis Wickes Hine, Library of Congress; *bottom*: author's collection.

First published 2023

Manufactured in the United States

ISBN 9781467151535

Library of Congress Control Number: 2023937178

Notice: The information in this book is true and complete to the best of our knowledge. It is offered without guarantee on the part of the author or The History Press. The author and The History Press disclaim all liability in connection with the use of this book.

*To every warrior whose life has been altered by cancer
and those who surrounded them with love and unconditional support.*

CONTENTS

ACKNOWLEDGEMENTS

As 2022 ended, I found myself exhausted and depleted. The entire year vanished as I experienced countless treatments and surgeries to rid my body of cancer. This meant delaying my book and not enjoying my greatest comfort: writing. So, first and foremost, I want to thank God for granting me life and strength and for guiding the hands of my surgeons, Dr. Kerry Perry and Dr. Bryce McKane.

I also want to thank The History Press and my editor, Ben Gibson, for their support and patience during this process. Despite the delays, they always placed my health above the due date.

I want to thank my family and friends, who are always my biggest cheerleaders and give up the most during the writing process. Cindi and Katerina, you are always my strength and my greatest blessings. Nothing, especially this past year and this book, would be possible without your consistent love and support. Tyrani and Kim, your friendships are what keep me sane and make me laugh on the dark days. To my work family, thank you for your continued support and allowing me to tell ghost stories about our building.

Thank you to the photographers who helped add depth to the stories. Without your artistic abilities, this project would not be complete.

Lastly, God bless Texas and all the ghosts who refuse to leave.

1

Introduction to Haunted North Central Texas

It is impossible to discuss Texas history without returning to the introduction of recognized human habitation in the state. The narrative regarding these occupants varies from storyteller to storyteller, with limited verifiable facts. Some claim the first people entered Texas around forty thousand years ago, arriving from the South. But a more significant number of historians say that this is not the case. They believe the Clovis people entered western Texas around 11,500 BC, making them the first to arrive. The Clovis hunted mammoth and bison with spears carved from native rock. Known as a Clovis point, the arrowhead is a thin, fluted projectile created by striking the edges of the stone with another stone. Long after the Clovis, other people came to the land to settle, as Texas offered water sources and flat ground for hunting, fishing and farming.

For years, Indigenous Americans retold stories for generations to instill lessons, recount the history of their people, keep their ancestors alive in the memories of all family members and entertain with folklore and legends. This strong tradition could play a role in the ceremony and mythology connecting Indigenous American culture to the spirit worlds. After all, their culture believes that spirits are potent and present in all natural items. There is no argument about the sacred nature of Indigenous American burial grounds. The desecration of graves creates angered spirits, and most people agree these spirits are best left at rest.

Caddo tribes covered much of northeastern Texas, Louisiana and southern portions of Arkansas and Oklahoma around AD 800. By AD 1200, they

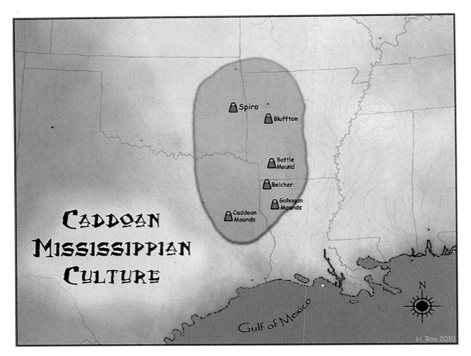

CADDOAN
MISSISSIPPIAN
CULTURE

Spiro
Bluffton
Battle Mound
Belcher
Gahagan Mounds
Caddoan Mounds

N

Gulf of Mexico

H. Roe 2010

The Caddo tribe dominated most of North Texas in the early years. *Herb Roe.*

had settled in the area now known as North Central Texas. They were the most advanced culture in Texas history to that point. The Caddo excelled in farming and agriculture and lived in well-built adobe-style homes. Caddoan is the traditional language of the Caddo Nation of Indigenous Americans. As of 2022, Caddoan is officially on the critically endangered list, as fewer than twenty-five people still speak the language. At least one word from the language will carry forward for many years to come. This dying language holds the history behind the name of the twenty-eighth U.S. state. The original name *Taysha* derives from Caddo and means "friend" or "ally." The spelling changed to "Teja" or "Texa," and Spanish explorers added the letter *s* to make it plural. Through these transitions, the name *Texas* was born with an Indigenous influence.

Texas passed through many hands before becoming a state. The phrase "six flags over Texas" signifies the six different entities that controlled a section of the territory during its formation. Spain, France, Mexico, the Republic of Texas, the United States and the Confederacy each ruled Texas at one point.

President Theodore Roosevelt visiting Fort Worth, Texas. *Library of Congress.*

The state of Texas has been represented by six different flags. Each flag represents the leadership of the area during a given time. *Author's collection.*

European exploration came, and the land drastically changed. Christopher Columbus first referred to Indigenous Americans as Indians. The term came about because Columbus was confident he had landed on one of the islands near the Indies. However, he was on American soil and meeting the first known Americans. These native individuals were the first to inhabit North America and Texas. Early Texas Natives were spear throwers and hunted large game animals for food and clothing. The land provided for them, and they replenished it by farming leafy vegetables and grains. They learned which foods were edible and added them to their diet as time passed. They advanced to bows and arrows, pottery, weaving and propagating crops such as maize. The Caddo enjoyed feasts, smoking tobacco, dancing, trading and negotiating. Although the new explorers introduced the Native Americans to horses, guns, metal pots, knives and axes, as more and more Europeans invaded the land, the Natives would not have time to celebrate or utilize these new tools. Instead, they found themselves forced to depart their land and go to other areas and states. The Caddo left behind several haunting stories that long to be shared and remembered.

The Caddo treated spirituality with the greatest respect and believed in a supreme god called the Caddi Ayo, loosely translated as "sky chief." Caddi Ayo created everything and everyone in the natural world. Humans, animals and plants are in touch with this supernatural force, and ghosts can appear in the form of deceased loved ones, familiar animals, monsters or demons. Spirits are invisible but lurk everywhere. These Caddo spirits floated through the state and lurked around every corner long before modern man.

The legend of Caddaja describes a horned, hideous, man-eating ogre who despises humans. The original story comes from an unpublished Spanish manuscript written by a friar, who describes his encounter with "the devil." The creature came from the bushes to attack two unsuspecting sisters. His eyes blazed red, and he exhibited tall horns and wings. He chased the sisters, capturing one sister who was pregnant and moved at a sluggish pace. He snatched her with his claws and forced her into his mouth as he devoured her flesh.

Another legend describes the sacred medicine water, which sounds like a visit to Mineral Wells, Texas. The Great Spirit enjoyed a good rest in an abundant forest filled with flowers, songbirds and small animals. One day, while he rested, a dragon devasted the land and brought disease and hunger to the people.

The people pleaded with the Great Spirit to subdue the dragon, and he did. He buried the dragon deep under the great mountains, and this is confirmed every time the earth shakes or lava and ash burst from a volcano.

The Great Spirit reclaimed his beautiful resting place, and as he rejoiced, he caused pure water to gush from the Earth. He asked that his favorite resting spot be a neutral ground where all could come to receive the healing waters. Still today, healing waters run through Mineral Wells and other locations for thousands to enjoy the healing properties of the water.

In 1520, Spain sent expeditions through Texas to search for a passage between the Gulf of Mexico and Asia. A map created by Álvarez de Pineda, the first Spanish explorer to reach the area, remains the earliest recorded document in Texas history. Although he claimed the land for Spain, the area was essentially ignored for over 160 years, leaving it open for the next European nation to stake a claim.

In 1682, French explorers claimed the entire Mississippi River valley. They constructed a fort and returned one of the ships to France to pass forward the news of their discovery. Their victory was short-lived. The Spanish learned of France venturing into Texas in 1685, prompting them to drive the French out.

Spain wished to regain control in Italy and their areas of interest in North America, including Texas. On January 23, 1691, Spain appointed the first governor to Texas, General Domingo Terán de Los Rios. By 1719, Spain and France were at war. The French found themselves leaving Texas without a single shot having been fired.

In 1821, Mexico fought to sever Spanish control of their land. They retrieved some ground for both Mexico and Texas. At the time, many enslaved people came to Texas under duress, and by 1825, there were 69 enslavers and 444 enslaved people residing in Texas. By 1836, there were well over 5,000 enslaved African Americans in Texas.

Finally, the time came for Texas to declare its independence. On March 2, 1836, the declaration created a new nation. This attempt at independence came when those in Texas felt heavy pressure to conform to Mexican laws and regulations. They signed the paper and effectively became the Republic of Texas. Even though Mexico refused to acknowledge Texas as an independent nation, Texas officials governed the republic. One of the first acts of the new republic was to overturn the Mexican prohibition of enslaved people and outlaw the emancipation of enslaved persons.

On February 28, 1845, the United States Congress narrowly passed a bill that authorized the annexation of Texas, making it an official state. While Texas had enjoyed the benefits of being its own nation, joining the United States provided additional allies against the Mexican government and protected Texas against further invasions from the South. The new state formed counties and elected officials to govern.

North Central Texas is used to describe the Dallas and Fort Worth Metroplex and surrounding area. It does not include the Panhandle of Texas, which expands farther north. The following counties encompass North Central Texas: Clay, Collin, Cooke, Dallas, Denton, Ellis, Erath, Fannin, Grayson, Hood, Hunt, Johnson, Kaufman, Montague, Navarro, Palo Pinto, Parker, Rockwell, Somervell, Tarrant and Wise.

With a history dating back to AD 800 and involving such unrest, it would not be far-fetched to believe that ghosts linger throughout Texas from coast to coast. The most haunted locations in the state remain around Dallas and Fort Worth, the exact area known as North Central Texas. The area includes not just Texan ghosts, but also Spanish, French, Mexican, Indigenous and African American ghosts.

2

HOME SWEET HAUNTED HOME

Imagine lying quietly in bed on a dark, moonless night. Texas-style thunder and lightning pause only long enough to acknowledge a power outage. There is no one else in the house, and the only sound is the snoring bulldog at the foot of the bed. Suddenly, the drop of heavy footsteps touches the stairs just outside the bedroom door. You are frozen in fear, and the security of the blankets appears the best sanctuary, as there is no easy escape. The steps grow louder and then suddenly stop just before the creak of the hinges on the door announces the intruder's entrance. The instinct of fight or flight rumbles to life. You toss the blankets aside and promptly switch on the bedside lamp. You look around the room with both fists raised, ready to rumble. But the room is silent and empty. There was no time for the uninvited guest to scamper away, and the room fell silent. These are the events seen on a Hollywood movie set, not in the average Joe's house. This event is an example of paranormal activity. But is the house haunted by a spirit?

This scenario is an example of a classic haunted house. The ghost manifests enough energy to create audible sounds of footsteps falling on the stairs and to open the bedroom door. A haunt in which a spirit can interact with its surroundings is a classic intelligent haunt. The ghost can recognize a closed door and open it. If the event plays much like a video recording in a residual haunt, the ghosts tend to walk through walls and doors. Although it may frighten its living occupant, most spirits do not intentionally scare the living. Some spirits are loved ones who passed on and now act as guardians.

It can also be a soul whose life ended abruptly, leaving the soul confused and lost. Those whose lives ended suspiciously might linger long enough to help the living solve the mystery surrounding their death or see the responsible criminal face justice. Some locations have more ghosts than others, and the comforts of a warm home go beyond life and death. Old, huge mansions often have former residents hanging around. Perhaps they are unwilling to part with their material goods, or maybe the homeless man from the alley several blocks away is trying to experience the good life. Whatever the case may be, haunted houses are the classic haunting grounds for your average, run-of-the-mill ghost.

THISTLE HILL MANSION (TARRANT COUNTY)

Daniel Waggoner was the eldest son of Solomon and Martha "Elizabeth" Waggoner from Tennessee. His father was a farmer and cattleman who dabbled in trading horses and enslaved people. Daniel moved from Tennessee to Texas with his parents, three brothers and five sisters at the ripe young age of twenty. Soon after the move, he married his first wife, Nancy Moore, in 1851 and moved to Wise County. A year later, the couple gave birth to a son, William Thomas "Tom" Waggoner. But Nancy would not live to see her son's second birthday. Daniel then married Sicily Halsell, the daughter of a prominent rancher. The couple did not have any additional children.

Daniel purchased over 520,000 acres of land near Vernon, Texas, under the name Dan Waggoner & Son. At the time, this large purchase spanned six counties and was the largest ranch in Texas. Tom Waggoner was only a teenager at the time, but he learned the ways of ranching from his father, who was successfully operating multiple farms. Father and son joined forces and established what would be known as the Waggoner Ranch after herding well over six thousand head of cattle to the land. The land provided ample opportunity to raise beef cattle, horses and crops. Daniel constructed a mansion in Decatur, Texas, in 1883. This Victorian-style home, called El Castille, became the focal point of the Waggoners' ranching business. In about 1903, the family drilled for water but made a startling discovery. They struck liquid gold when black oil gushed from the hole. The Waggoners profited from this supplementary revenue.

In 1877, Tom married Ella Halsell, the younger sister of his stepmother, Sicily. Tom helped his father with the ranch, but he kept busy with other

Electra Waggoner received Thistle Hill mansion as a gift from her father. He hoped to keep his only daughter close to his home. *QuesterMark.*

adventures. He was the founder and president of Waggoner National Bank, established Arlington Downs and paid for constructing three buildings at Texas Woman's University. Years later, he received an award from Fort Worth for the honorary title of "First Citizen of Fort Worth."

In 1882, Ella gave birth to the couple's only daughter, Electra. The firstborn and only daughter of the wealthy rancher instantly became Tom's favorite.

In 1883, Ella gave birth to the couple's first son, Guy. The couple's second son, Edward "Paul," was born six years later. Ella kept busy with the children while Tom prepared for their future. The ranch, the mansion and the enormous business empire landed in Tom's hands after Daniel passed away in 1902.

The already affluent family had an abundance of money to spare. But bickering, backstabbing and divorce began to overshadow the magnificent mansion, herds of cattle and horses and oil glistening in the hot Texas sun. Tom was fifty-seven in 1909, and on Christmas Day, he divided the large ranch into four separate tracts, keeping one for himself and gifting the other three to his children. Tom asked each of his children to draw cards to determine which parcel of land they would receive. He secretly hoped that his daughter would draw the property closest to him, and when she didn't, he declared a redraw. The fixed card game and uneven distribution of land

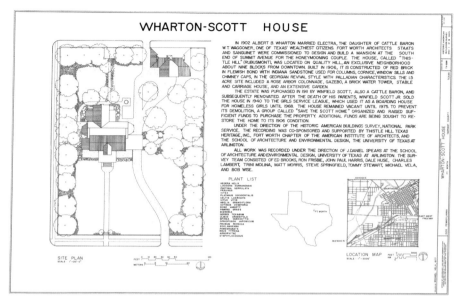

Opposite, top: The brick exterior of Thistle Hill mansion is accented with exquisite, large white pillars. *QuesterMark.*

Opposite, bottom: Fencing and a strong gate block the home from the surrounding streets and buildings. *QuesterMark.*

Above: Original plans for the mansion's layout and design show the lush vegetation surrounding the home. *Historic American Buildings Survey, Library of Congress.*

started a family quarrel. While he intended for each child to take over a part of the family business, the spoiled, wealthy siblings blew through money and neglected the business. In 1923, Tom knew he had protected the ranch's future by reclaiming the land and assets and placing them in a trust.

Thistle Hill mansion is a three-story Georgian Revival structure built for Electra Waggoner in 1903. Electra's father gifted the estate to her at her wedding to Albert Warton. He knew this would keep his favorite child close and under his watchful eye. She, like her siblings, favored the finer things in life and liked to spend money. Electra enjoyed shopping for luxury items and could run up a Neiman Marcus tab of over $20,000 in one shopping trip. She lived life to the fullest, throwing extravagant parties, and reports stated that she came home from a journey with a butterfly tattoo on her leg. Her lifestyle took a toll on her health, and she passed away at the early age of forty-three from cirrhosis of the liver. The party was over. But some believe she never left her mansion and is still roaming the halls.

Renovation in 1970 turned up at least two apparitions floating through the mansion's halls. Visitors feel one ghost is a woman seen on the grand staircase dressed in white. The other is a male in tennis clothes and sporting a handlebar mustache. The mustache man could be the spirit of Winfield Scott, who died unexpectedly just before the renovations reached completion. Scott purchased the home from Waggoner. During this time, workers also heard music emanating from the ballroom on the third floor, which had been closed. Voices and footsteps commonly fill the quiet.

A paranormal investigation in 1997 turned up disembodied voices and footsteps. It also discovered that a ninety-seven-year-old rocking chair in the ballroom moved of its own accord. The investigators covered the chair in plastic and removed it from the ballroom. But they later found the chair back in the ballroom and uncovered despite everyone present acknowledging they had moved the chair.

During the writing process, it is common for an author to connect with specific topics or chapters of the book. For this book, Electra Waggoner stood out to me. She passed away on November 26, and my birthdate is November 26. When I shared her photos with friends and family, they noted a resemblance with me. As COVID calms down and the museum reopens, it will be interesting to see if there is still a connection inside the mansion where she resided.

BAKER MANSION (PARKER COUNTY)

In 1890, John Baker went into business with George Poston to open a dry-goods store in Weatherford, Texas. It was a gamble, but it paid off. This business venture would grow into a chain of stores. Baker also directed the Crystal Palace Flouring Mill, was president of the First National Bank and helped establish Weatherford College. The business was lucrative and enabled Baker to build a seven-thousand-square-foot Victorian mansion for his growing family. Baker and his wife, Alice, had four children by 1894. The children were Alice "Ethel," Harry, Charles and Mary. While John's business profited, not all was well at the Baker estate. The first of many tragedies struck the family in 1894.

Ethel fell ill and did not show signs of improvement. After a long and painful illness, she passed away before completing the mansion. Unfortunately, she would not be the only Baker to die before the home's completion. On Easter

Sunday 1899, John Baker died at age fifty-one, at the height of his success as a businessman.

Construction finished in 1904, and Alice Baker moved into the lush home with her three surviving children, but luck and health fell victim to the Baker family curse. Four years after moving into the house, Charles left the family home on a business trip. Charles was intelligent and frequently traveled as a buyer of the Baker Poston Dry Goods Company. He had health issues impacting his walking and general well-being, but nothing so serious as to keep him from working the family business. He traveled from San Francisco to Seattle before he vanished without a trace. The family hired private investigators and even offered a $5,000 reward for the return of Charles's body, dead or alive.

Meanwhile, Harry continued to travel for the company, and in 1924, he found himself in Chicago with a ruptured appendix. He barely escaped death. Mary decided it was time to declare Charles officially dead in 1936. Sadly, this was another death in the Baker family.

Mary sold the mansion to the president of the First National Bank, George Fant, in the early 1940s. George had two children with his first wife. One child succumbed to a ruptured appendix at age seven. His other child, Knox, was piloting a military aircraft in 1942 when it crashed during a training mission. Knox died on impact. The Fant family absorbed the house's curse as they took ownership.

Fant longed for company and remarried, to a woman named Elena. When he passed away in 1962, Elena remained in the mansion. The ghost stories began when her niece came to visit. In accounts of the tale, storytellers redacted the niece's name for privacy. In this book, she is Betty.

During the renovation in the 1940s, the home came to life—or afterlife. Betty often visited her aunt at the mansion and utilized the time to write in her journal. Fearing ridicule, she kept her stories private. It was through these journals that her ghost story came to life.

She began writing in the journals after everyone was sound asleep; Betty heard footsteps in the hallway between her aunt's room and her own. As the footsteps came closer to her room, she closed her eyes tightly, frightened of what might appear. Neither of the women in the home had the ability to struggle against an intruder. When Betty gathered her bravery, she opened her eyes to find a shadowy figure standing at the foot end of her bed, prompting a bloodcurdling scream from Betty. The sound in the hall had not come from an intruder but from something paranormal. The shadow disappeared. Betty refused to stay the night for a long time and did not share the story with anyone. She kept her encounter sealed in the pages of her journal.

Twenty years later, the night before her wedding, Betty returned to stay with her aunt. She was resting in her bed and reading a book when she heard a loud cry. Fearing her aunt had fallen out of bed, she raced to her aid but found her aunt sound asleep. Betty continued to search for the source of the noise. In the dining room, she found the maid in a frightened state and pointing at a giant bat that had crashed into the sliding glass door and was now lying dead on the floor. Betty felt relief that her aunt was not injured, and the event did not seem paranormal.

In the mid-1960s, Betty was out shopping in town when she struck up a conversation with a store clerk about the Baker mansion. The clerk reported a story about an event in the 1920s when Mrs. Baker threw a large party. During the party, loud noise alerted everyone, who rushed to find that it came from an old armoire that had belonged to the long-lost brother, Charles Baker. The armoire door opened independently, and an old, starched collar rolled past the guests, landing on the exact spot where the maid had discovered the dead bat. Now the innocent bat's death took a strange, paranormal turn in Betty's mind.

Betty, despite her fear, moved into the home with her husband when the couple purchased it from Mrs. Fant. Betty's husband often worked late and traveled on business, leaving Betty and Mrs. Fant alone in the large, empty estate. Mrs. Fant remained in the home until 1970, when she moved to a smaller home next door. Betty's ghostly visitations resumed after about one year of living in the home.

Ghost sightings did not happen daily but occurred several more times over the years while Betty lived in the home. One night, she noted a shadow in the stairwell moving toward her bedroom and approaching her bed. She then felt a gentle hand rest on her shoulder. Perhaps this was the same ghost from her childhood, but Betty did not feel the same fear. Her fears decreased, and although Betty knew the invisible visitor constantly watched her, she did not feel that the spirit had malicious intent. Still, something about it held the potential for unfriendly interactions.

The worst incident happened in the spring of 1976. Betty was alone, and the night brought a predictable Texas thunderstorm. The strong winds took out the power. She heard a loud pounding coming from the basement door. With the door constantly secured and it being the only entrance inside the home, Betty figured the wind rattled something, making a knocking noise. She phoned her aunt next door, who agreed to meet her between the homes. The pounding stopped as Betty ran past the basement door, but the volume increased as the frightened woman exited the house. From that night forward, she could not find consolation in the home.

Betty believed the ghost was that of Charles Baker, the missing son, returning home. She also felt Charles did not like her being in his home or perhaps did not understand her presence in the Baker mansion. Over the years, others have encountered Charles, but none quite as profoundly as Betty.

BURLESON HOME (TRAVIS COUNTY)

Thomas Burleson left his comfortable job at the district attorney's office to venture into the honeybee business. In 1903, Burleson purchased five dollars' worth of honeybees and fifteen dollars' worth of honey-making supplies. Three years later, Burleson received a colony of bees and established his company in 1907. He formed his headquarters at his farmhouse. Burleson sold pure Texas honey and promptly became one of the top ten honey brands in the United States. The company's success

The Burleson home is the original headquarters for Burleson Honey. *Wiki Commons.*

25

allowed for construction of a two-story, three-thousand-square-foot home with a guest house in the back. Minor setbacks affected the bee farm through the years. In 1923, a fire destroyed over half of the production. But in 1929, Burleson's son joined the business, and it continued to show success as they purchased their first long-haul truck in 1935 and moved to bigger headquarters in 1936.

In 1944, Burleson crossed the street to visit an ailing friend. An automobile struck him, causing instant death. The company lived on through his son and remained strong, but some believe he may still be buzzing around in the Burleson home.

The current owners, Angel and Kimberly Quintero, moved into the home in October 2011. Thankfully, the duo had a curiosity about the paranormal and were not frightened by stories they heard or events they experienced. The Quinteros state that lights often flickered off and on, the doors slammed on their own accord and unexplained cold spots floated in the air. They also report smelling cigar smoke in the stairway. They have captured many paranormal events on video and shared them via YouTube.

Other visitors and former residents reported seeing a male figure smoking a cigar at the top of the stairs, which matches the story by the owners. It is possible that Burleson smoked a cigar, as smoke calms bees.

CROZIER-SICKLES HOUSE (COLLIN COUNTY)

In 1893, John Crozier died, leaving his widow, Nannie, with three daughters, Mary Annie, Emma and Lula. Nannie was a strong and independent woman who wanted the best for her children despite the loss of their father. In 1895, she had a home built for her family. The formidable mother supervised the cultivation of the land and broke ground in areas previously untouched. She even homeschooled her children. Lula died from typhoid just five years after builders completed the home.

In 1977, the Crozier family sold the home to John and Donna Sickles. The ghostly adventures began after they moved into the house. The couple often noted glimpses of "something" out of the corner of their eyes. They heard noises in the hallway, followed by a knee-high shadow entering the room. At other times, they saw a small gray cat in the hallway mirror and heard bumps in the night. All photos taken in the hallway appeared to have a haze over them. Photos taken in other areas seemed uneventful and ghost-free. Paranormal activity heightened when remodeling began but did seem to lessen when construction was completed.

The Sickles couple saw mist-like specters that disappeared in the blink of an eye. They often woke to the sound of knocking, which occurred at all hours of the night and day, making it difficult to rest in peace.

During the era of the home's original construction, builders often held a superstition that an upside down baluster helped keep ghosts from ascending the stairs. This action did not help the Sickles family. They noted that the staircase's seventh baluster fitted in the slot upside down during the remodel.

Visitors report hearing voices and singing, seeing shadows and feeling as if they are not alone while touring the home. The Sickles family donated the home to Frisco Heritage Center in 2002, and the center moved it from its original location in 2006. The question remained: Did the ghosts stay behind or come with the home?

The house is currently located in the Frisco Heritage Center and stands among twelve other structures. There is a jail, a log cabin, a railroad depot and even an old church, but most agree that the Crozier-Sickles house is the most haunted dwelling.

HAUNTED HILL HOUSE (KAUFMAN COUNTY)

No, this is not the one portrayed in the Hollywood movies, but it is one of the spookier homes in Texas. At one time, the home supplied working girls to the Baker Hotel, and it had seven reported deaths and possibly nine ghosts. Locals believe those who died in the home never left.

The direct ties to the hotel left this home to host bootleggers, prostitutes and a secret gambling den for those wishing to remain discreet. Built in 1880 by one of Mineral Wells' founding families, the house served as a makeshift hospital until 1929.

The house is a hot spot for paranormal activity and attracts television shows and investigators from around the world. *TAPS, Haunted Collector, Ghost Adventures, Deep South Paranormal, Paranormal Files, Portals to Hell, Strangetown* and Christopher Saint Booth have all sought to connect with the spirits in the haunted hill house. Brave individuals can tour the home, do overnight investigations and rent the venue for weddings and birthdays. Only 50 percent of those who attempt to spend the night at this haunted location stay until morning. This statistic includes professional paranormal investigators.

Katherine Estes and her husband, Eddie, saw the house as an exciting investment. The couple enjoyed an excellent paranormal investigation and often visited Jefferson, Texas, to explore haunted locations and participate in the ghost walks. During a visit to Jefferson, a paranormal investigator showed the Esteses a photo from the haunted hill house. The image appeared to show two boys and one girl playing together in a room. The children seemed to be transparent. A haunted home was waiting for the right buyer to purchase it. A year later, they saw the house price drop by $100,000.

No severe injuries line the pages of reported attacks, but when the house was on the real estate market, thirty-nine people received scratches when visiting it. Others received bite marks, were pushed and even tripped when walking through the house.

While most potential buyers flee from paranormal activity, Katherine and Eddie placed a bid to buy the home, saying that the house called to them. In 2017, they finalized the sale and became the proud owners of a home that still held at least nine former occupants.

Many of the ghosts are young children, possibly children of the former working girls who lived in the house. Not all of the ghosts are friendly.

One of the most powerful entities in the house could be a young boy. It is reported that John Henry Kyle was the son of one of the hill house's working girls. Born with several deformities, the boy passed away at about six years of age. The previous owner, paleontologist Phil Kirchoff, called this ghost Joshua and believed that he had Down Syndrome. No one is certain of his cause of death.

Kirchoff said that he often heard a voice clearly say, "I'm Joshua."

One spirit is of a girl named Madeleine, believed to nine years old. The girl suffered fatal injuries when struck by an automobile on the road. Observers of her accident brought her petite body to the house's front porch, where she was pronounced dead.

Kirchoff also reported that two mediums visited the house, both stopping in the same spot. Enclosed behind drywall was an old bathroom directly behind a new bathroom. The old bathroom held a claw-foot tub, a sink and a toilet. The two mediums reported the same findings. They felt a woman sitting on the bathroom floor holding a deceased infant. The mediums felt that both mother and child failed to survive a complicated birthing process.

A previous owner fell down a well and remained there until officials located his dead body. Another death story involves a nine-year-old boy found hanging from a tree in the backyard.

Reportedly inhabited by nine ghosts, this house may be the most haunted in Texas. The current owners welcome visitors but advise using extreme caution. And no matter how tempting, the Esteses do not recommend taking any items home, as ghosts may be attached.

3
OCCUPATIONAL HAZARDS

Paranormal investigators agree that unfinished business is one of the most common reasons a soul might linger. Spirits who pass away suddenly, violently or in an untimely manner might find it hard to accept that they are dead. These ghosts will usually disappear if informed of their "condition." Some ghosts want to assist in locating their killer and will appear only to those who can solve the mystery. These spirits might move on when the case closes and their killer is behind bars. Some ghosts stick around to say goodbye to a loved one.

On November 6, 2002, nodding off to sleep proved effortless for me. But, in the early morning hours, something unusual occurred. I woke to the most potent scent of my grandmother's perfume. I drifted back to dreamland with heavy eyelids and underwent an unforgettable experience. There was a large ballroom filled with dancers and partygoers. Among the crowd were familiar faces, and while moving in unison, a group approached. Grandma extended her arms for a hug as tears fell on warm, blushed cheeks. Grandpa appeared as a slightly older version of my father and looked radiant in his black tuxedo and shined dress shoes.

"Do not be sad," Grandma began. "Grandpa is here and the rest of the family. They all came."

Their faces beamed with smiles as they approached. Seeing Grandma with them did not make sense, as the other family members had passed away many years prior.

"Look at this dress." Grandma twirled around in a royal blue ball gown that highlighted her sapphire eyes. Her light brown hair bounced in a full array

This photo depicts the author's paternal grandparents around the time of their wedding. *Author's collection.*

of curls. "With a thin body and strong bones, dancing is possible again. Isn't it wonderful?"

As quick as they had appeared, the people disappeared, and a ringing telephone broke the quietness of the morning.

Now fully awake, I picked up the phone to find my mother on the line, "Grandma passed away early this morning."

Disbelief filled my soul when I recalled my dream and learned that Grandma loved ballroom dancing and excelled at it until her worn-out body prevented her from a good tango or foxtrot. I remember watching ballroom dancing on the television but did not know she was a dancer.

Ghosts stick around because they want to and can. Tricksters continue playing tricks, evildoers continue to cause trouble, helpers continue to help and some dedicated employees continue to clock in for their shifts. Haunted businesses tend to be in old buildings that have been renovated or in places where someone has experienced a tragic death. Next time the cashier seems aloof or the waiter is slow as molasses, consider that they might not be among the living.

UNDERTAKER BUILDING (JOHNSON COUNTY)

When creating a nonfiction masterpiece, it is exciting to stumble on a story that screams to be shared. An average historic three-story brick building in Cleburne, Texas, screamed for consideration.

Recent newspaper articles drew attention to this location and drew my interest to delve deeper into the history. Vincent Gray founded a small hardware and undertaking business near Camp Henderson (modern-day Cleburne). It was common for an undertaker to build the coffins and bury the dead. In 1868, he moved the business to 114 East Chambers Street, and this building still stands in the historic downtown district.

The Deering company was one of the first recognized embalmers in the state of Texas. It was first owned by Tobe Blackwell, and then Reola Deering in 1894. Deering started his career as a civil engineer. He then tried mechanics, firefighting and finally undertaking. He met and married Effie Gray, daughter of Vincent Gray. The couple had a son named Vincent and named the company D.H. Deering and Son when young Vincent joined the family business. Gray died in 1897 at the age of sixty-four, and the business changed hands.

The building design allowed a proper memorial. A stage rests on the second floor, where tearful visitors once mourned their loved ones in a remembrance funeral service. Historian Mary Tadsen suggests that the stage held performances with a much different flair after the undertakers moved out. At some point in history, the building became a gentlemen's club, with women performing striptease acts on the stage and entertaining men with other services for the right price.

Frank Garza purchased the building to operate Garza's Famous Chigo Hot Dogs. He is the gentleman interviewed in the newspaper articles detailing the mysterious items left behind by the former occupants as well as the strange occurrences. One news channel deemed the building a "theater of strange."

In 2010, the actual head of the beloved mascot Chico turned up missing. Someone stole the statue's head and dared to send a ransom request to *Cleburne Times-Review* worker Matt Smith. But the ransom note was not for Chico's head. Instead, the letter's author claimed to be holding a historical photo album stolen from the location. Shortly after moving into the building, Garza's son Casey found a photo album in the attic containing landmark photos dating to the 1800s. The ransom request offered to return the photo album if Garza served up payment. The ransom demanded one hundred free hot dogs on Valentine's Day. Eager for the return of the album, Garza agreed to the demands. He then donated the recovered photo album to the historical society in Cleburne.

Strange events continued to befall this location. On one occasion, Garza met a man who asked to look around the building. The man stated that he had worked in the building many years before. When they reached the third floor, the man grew somber and stopped in his tracks. He explained that he had witnessed a young man delivering drinks to a group of men playing poker. Suddenly, for no reason, one of the men grabbed the young boy and threw him down the stairs. The boy fell to the second-floor landing, where he lay motionless. The incident did not make news, and the body disappeared without a trace. If the boy died from injuries sustained in the fall, his aggressor covered his tracks well enough to hide the crime.

It was the third floor that initially enticed Garza. While exploring, he found a large, beveled mirror on the wall. It was captivating, and Garza

Cleburne's town square shown during a busy farmers market. *Library of Congress.*

instantly decided he wanted to detach the mirror and bring it home to be displayed and viewed. He undid the clips holding the mirror in place and began to pry it from the wall, using extreme caution to prevent breaking the antique. Despite his efforts, the mirror did not budge. He could see no adhesive, but Garza felt the mirror must have been attached with glue and decided to leave it where he found it. He reattached the clips and walked away. Two weeks later, Garza found the mirror shattered in a thousand pieces on the ground. He checked the back of the mirror and the wall for adhesive but found no trace.

Garza stated, "The pieces of the mirror landed far away from the location where it hung on the wall, and all of the pieces were facing up."

Visitors and occupants noted that the lamps in the building turned on and off on their own and that light bulbs often exploded despite upgraded electricity in the building. Unaided footsteps and muted voices lingered in the building. The scent of perfume lingered around the second floor.

The building made the newspaper again when Fire Chief Clint Ishmael noted that the old building was leaning, and he was concerned about a few protruding bricks. He used his resources to make his way to the loose bricks, and when he pulled one out, he found thousands of tiny eyes staring back at him. Bats filled the entire wall. Their droppings froze and then thawed over the years, creating tension and movement with the bricks.

Today, the hot dog business is closed, but the stories of the first undertaker and his building make visitors wonder if Vincent Gray is still open for business.

The Catfish Plantation (Ellis County)

It is always challenging to tell a ghost story that's already known. Sometimes, the facts vary from storyteller to storyteller. One crucial aspect is utilizing known and verifiable information of an account to shed light on the details. This section, on the Catfish Plantation, will be told via shared stories on the internet and articles from history that complement the mysterious origins.

The 1895 Victorian home at 814 Water Street in Waxahachie displays a "gingerbread house inspired look," with its resemblance to the famous cookie construction. The home's first owner is said to have been a farmer with the last name Anderson. There is disagreement about his name, but it is essential to remember that different researchers will locate different information. Through research, it was found that a man with the last name Anderson and two women named Elizabeth had ties to vital details of the ghost stories of this location.

At least three ghosts are said to still reside at 814 Water Street. The first is a young woman named Elizabeth. Elizabeth first appeared during a séance led by Ruth Jones. During the séance, the walls knocked, dishes rattled and the candle in the middle of the table burst into a bright light. The kitchen doors flew open, and a young woman in a wedding-style gown stood in the room. The scent of roses filled the air. This sparked the story of Elizabeth, who was the daughter of farmer Anderson. Elizabeth was believed to have died by murder in the home in the early 1920s. Her ex-boyfriend rushed into the building on her wedding day and, in a jealous rage, strangled her to death.

Research revealed a young woman named Mary Elizabeth Anderson Gammon, who lived in Waxahachie in the 1920s. She was the daughter of Ezekiel and Elizabeth Anderson. She died on October 8, 1907, at the age of thirty-three. She was married to Robert Gammon at the time of her death.

The couple lost an infant in 1898. Her death at a young age leaves open the possibility that she was the victim of murder at the hands of an ex-lover or suffered another tragic death.

Elizabeth visits the dining room, where she likes to reach out and touch customers. She is considered a gentle spirit who fills the air with a rose scent and appears in a beautiful, flowing dress.

The next ghost believed to stumble around the Catfish Plantation is Caroline. Research reveals that a woman named Carrie Jenkins Mooney lived in the home from the 1950s until her death on December 23, 1970, at eighty years of age. During her life, Carrie enjoyed cooking and was frequently found in the kitchen, as she is today. Carrie, or Caroline, is a grumpy spirit who likes to stir up trouble. She, like many women of her time, despised alcoholic beverages. Staff had to place the wine glasses behind the protective glass of a large armoire, as the ghost broke many wine glasses.

One of the previous owners reported the smell of freshly brewed coffee as she began her morning routine in the restaurant. She later found a large iced-tea urn in the middle of the kitchen floor filled with coffee cups.

The third spirit may be a man in overalls who goes by the name of Will. He was a farmer who died in the building. There are mixed reports of whether he died of natural causes or from a sickness. He is reticent but does love to grab the legs of female diners. Local police have received reports of a man sitting on the front porch in overalls. When they arrive, he disappears before they can exit their patrol cars.

The beautiful gingerbread home draws visitors for the delicious food and hauntingly good atmosphere.

THE CELT IRISH PUB (COLLIN COUNTY)

Located in McKinney, Texas, the Tuck Hill House was a known hideout for Frank and Jesse James. The original owner, Francis Marion "Tuck" Hill, was a second cousin to the legendary duo. The cousins reportedly created a sanctuary in the attic of the home. Though Frank and Jesse committed no robberies in McKinney, they made the town their own. They enjoyed a good night out on the town, gambling and drinking at local saloons.

Long before it was the Celt Irish Pub, a saloon stood on the property. In the early 1800s, a brothel occupied the site. The original bar contained trapdoors and secret exits to assist patrons with quick getaways when police

Lunchtime on a cotton farm in McKinney, Texas, in 1913. *Lewis Wickes Hine, Library of Congress.*

knocked on the door. Due to the sketchy clientele, several shootouts took place near the building.

There is video evidence of glasses being knocked over, and strange noises fill the recorders of investigators. Cold spots are felt throughout the building, and forks keep turning up, stuck in furniture and on the walls. There was enough action to pique the interest of a local paranormal team.

Paranormal investigators collected multiple electronic voice phenomena (EVPs) during the investigation.

"I need a fork," said a young male voice.

"Y'all are crazy," said another male voice.

"I hate dancing," said a female voice.

4

SCHOOL SPIRIT

Upper-level college students are known to tell tall tales to frighten incoming students, and rumors can spread through dorms like wildfire. It is hard to make up an original, believable story. At times, though, the generation before did the work. Stories need to convince the newcomers that the strange knocks in the night are not because the building is over one hundred years old. Those noises come from Janitor Fred, who tragically died when his broom handle got stuck in the elevator shaft, or from Becky, who tried to hide her pregnancy and perished alone while giving birth. If all school hauntings are fictional, why do they seem so real? The explanation is spookier than the stories created for fright.

Old newspapers can be challenging to navigate, and the challenge increases when there are no clear facts, such as a victim's name or age or even when the event occurred. For example, one college has the story of a female student who died during childbirth. The incident originated in the college's early days, when the dorm was an all-female residence and an unwed mother was not acceptable. But the woman's name and the year it happened remain unknown. Unraveling the mystery would require hours of research. The family and the college would benefit if the story failed to appear in newspapers. Maybe this is what the upper-level students bank on?

The COVID pandemic increased stress on students of all ages, and the suicide rate rose. The American College Health Association reports that the suicide rate among young adults aged fifteen to twenty-four has tripled since

1950, and suicide is currently the second-most-common cause of death among college students. For many of these young adults, it is their first time away from home, they have bills to pay and failing a class can destroy the chance to graduate and obtain a good job. College is also a time to date and meet potential mates. Dating itself is a dangerous sport, and heartbreak can lead to depression.

Not all scary school stories come from the creative minds of those wishing to experience fear. Many are based on true stories and have proof of their facts. Others lack evidence but continue for many generations until they become legends.

WOODMEN'S CIRCLE HOME (GRAYSON COUNTY)

In Sherman, Texas, sits a large, red-brick building on fifteen acres of land. Built by the Woodmen's Insurance Company in the mid-1920s, this site served as an orphanage for children in need and a dorm for widowed women. Dora Alexander Talley, one of the founders, was the driving force behind the orphanage, dorm and school for women and children. She envisioned a place for widowed or retired insurance company members to care for children in need. The space provided homes for well over 100 children and around 165 widowed women at any given time.

In 1927, the Supreme Woodmen acquired land to construct a home for widows and orphans. The organization provided food, shelter, clothing, recreation and education for single and widowed women in exchange for caring for the children as if they were their own. This plan benefited all parties. The well-kept grounds and the well-maintained home came from the company's money and was sufficient to keep everyone comfortable. Other orphanages were rumored to mistreat the young children in their care; this was not the case for Woodmen's Circle.

Woodmen's Circle operated until 1971. The site then experienced a series of unfortunate events. The home itself was falling apart and was not up to proper building codes.

From 1977 to 1981, the main building was leased to Reverend Ariel Sherman and the Good Shepherd Tabernacle Church, who turned the location into a commune. Local rumors said that this was not an average church and that Reverend Sherman was running a satanic cult. Members of the same church at a location in Oregon found themselves in a legal battle as a result of the mistreatment of children. This legal action prompted locals to believe in the cult theory after Reverend Sherman's church reported the death of a four-year-old child. The rumors were that a young boy fell down the shaft of a dumbwaiter and died. Sherman also faced child-abuse charges after a fifteen-year-old girl from the congregation died of cancer. She was said to have had a tumor the size of a basketball. The girl's mother sided with Sherman and opted for prayer over conventional medical care. Soon after, the church closed.

The home stood empty for several years and became an attractive vandalism target. A series of fires threatened to destroy the property and damage multiple buildings. In 1990, a private party purchased the property. Although the owners have not restored the buildings, they are protecting and preserving the remaining buildings with barbed-wire fencing and "no trespassing" signs.

People have reported seeing strange lights coming from the buildings and surrounding land. Those who visited the facilities when they were open to the public reported seeing strange shadows, hearing unexplainable noises and feeling uneasy. Later, those who photographed the buildings found faces peering out of windows and strange orbs floating through the photos.

One investigator, Ken Kemp, was allowed to explore the home. He had obtained permission from the current owners. After receiving a firm warning to be aware of the decay and damage to the buildings, he set out to explore.

A former employee took him on a tour of the grounds, and she stated that neither she nor anyone she worked with had experienced any paranormal events. She had worked in the buildings during the short time they housed a nursing home with many bedridden patients. As a general feeling, Kemp suggested that remaining spirits might come from the number of orphans and women who called this place home. Many resided here until their deaths, and their bodies remained on the land.

Those who grew up in Sherman will tell the stories of this location for years to come.

Hill School (Tarrant County)

Built in 1960, the original school operated without conflicts and for a brief time ceased operation in 2013. During the initial remodel of the school, the headmaster, Kathy Edwards, was surveying the building from outside when she made a startling discovery. She noticed a large hole, big enough for a casket, which left her wondering what the ground held before the school was built. It was after this initial remodel that paranormal activity sparked.

Reportedly, the middle stall in the girl's bathroom has a door that opens and slams on its own and with no one nearby. The security cameras and alarms go off at all hours of the day and night. But there is no evidence of human or animal interaction when investigated. Late-night workers report footsteps and voices and see dark shadows and strange lights.

In 2014, the school reopened under a different name.

Newman High School (Dallas County)

Newman High School is a public high school for Carrolton and Farmer's Branch and opened in 1975. Its name comes from a former superintendent, Newman Smith.

While there is no concrete evidence to support the stories of paranormal activity at this school, many students have experienced ghostly encounters and even interacted with spirits.

The story begins in the theater, where a female student named Abigail is said to have passed away. Abigail was attempting to store boxes on the stage when she died. She continues to walk the catwalk.

Students have experimented with hitting the stage with a hammer three times to let Abigail know when they need her to not interfere with their performances. She walks into the shadows and remains there until the end of the performance.

Texas Woman's University (Denton County)

In 1901, the Texas Industrial Institute and College for White Girls of the State of Texas in Arts and Science founded a public institution in Denton. The name did not roll off the tongue. Two years later, the name became Girls' Industrial College. It had a dual mission that dates to the origination of the school and stands strong today. That mission is to provide a liberal education and to prepare women "for the practical industries of the age" with a specialization in education. While the mission and the name catered

While Texas Woman's University started with a goal of educating women, men have been admitted since. *Library of Congress.*

to women, the university began admitting men in 1972. But 90 percent of the student population remains female. Several name changes occurred until Texas Woman's University (TWU) was settled on in 1957.

It can be challenging to distinguish a true ghost story from a false report at a university. After all, a good portion of freshman year involves students learning the tall tales and spooky stories from upper-level students. TWU is no different. Suicides and tragic deaths have led to possible hauntings and lingering spirits.

Distant voices and moaning fill the halls in the building known as "Old Main." This building was the first one constructed and has been around since 1903. Visitors to the building find a headless statue titled *Winged Victory*, which can be daunting to encounter. The moaning and barely audible voices belong to faculty who are still coming to work each day to teach and to students still wishing to learn. The first ghost story circulated just months after the building opened. At midnight, music played throughout the building. Students attempted to solve the mystery, but the music stopped when students lit a match and a gas lamp to illuminate the room. They found the building to be empty. Sometime later, a student confessed to playing the music and hiding. The discovery did not calm everyone's nerves,

In 1903, Old Main served as the sole instructional building for the Girls' Industrial College of Texas. *Author's collection.*

and people have a feeling of unease when visiting Old Main. A few blamed the prankster, but most believe ghosts haunt the structure.

One of the most interesting buildings on campus is the chapel, known as the "Little Chapel in the Woods." Constructed in 1939, the chapel was dedicated by TWU to Eleanor Roosevelt. The primary design work, including stained-glass windows, art, flooring and lighting, was undertaken by TWU students. With the amount of heart and soul inside this small building, it is easy to see how it could impact people in both life and death. Over the years, countless couples said, "I do" in the chapel. But at least one wedding did not go quite as planned. Legend tells of a woman's husband jilting her at the altar and the woman ending her life by jumping from the second story.

Students named the forever bride the "hooded bride." She now finds herself roaming the grounds around the chapel wearing a white flowing dress. This tale has been around since at least the 1950s, but there is no documented evidence of a death at the chapel.

"I have looked into this, and there is actually no death record of the Hooded Bride at TWU," Little Chapel in the Woods coordinator Brittany Jasper states.

Jasper did admit that one can feel the energy during special weddings, and sometimes candles will blow out on their own despite no air circulating. She does feel that the energy is warm and welcoming, rather than sorrowful and dark. She also reports the sound of footsteps falling on the staircase when no one is present.

One witness stated that she said her vows in the chapel and felt nothing but comfort and peace. She felt the love shown in the walls and stained-glass windows, making it the perfect location for a blessed wedding.

Deaths were and are usually hidden from the public as much as possible when it comes to public schools. After all, dorm rooms are cramped enough without the addition of a possible ghost or two residing there. A few deaths have been recorded at TWU and could lend some truth to possible spirits haunting the university.

Guinn Hall serves as a residence hall on campus and is visible from most points in the city, as it is the tallest building in Denton. Around 2000, a female student allegedly jumped from the ninth-story balcony and died on impact. However, there is no evidence of this event happening, except the closure of access to the balconies at Guinn Hall. Many believe the school closed the balconies to prevent future falls. Some students and staff believe that Dr. John Guinn, the man for whom Guinn Hall is named, is the ghostly voice and shadow figure seen floating around the building.

Left: More than three hundred students in the fine arts department contributed to the art in the Little Chapel. *Author's collection*.

Opposite: Guinn Hall stands twenty-four stories tall and was named for the sixth president of the campus, John Guinn. *Author's collection*.

In 2015, a female student named Brenna Taylor fell victim to a hit-and-run accident when walking along Bell Avenue, near the outskirts of the university. Brenna was a senior at TWU majoring in interdisciplinary studies. She might be one of the friendly spirits attending classes at the university in hopes of finishing her degree.

Tragic news struck the university in 2016, when reports of a missing student flooded the media. Police found twenty-four-year-old Jaqueline "Jackie" Vandagriff's lifeless body charred by fire. As they pieced together the events, police learned that Vandagriff had just met Charles Bryant. There was no way for her to know he had been stalking TWU and the University of North Texas (UNT) with his eyes on his former girlfriend, Caitlin Mathis, who attended UNT. Mathis had been struggling to keep away from Bryant. She had him arrested three times and even filed a restraining order, which kept him away from her and the TWU campus. Police were able to bring Bryant in for questioning when he violated the restraining order and contacted Mathis just days after Vandagiff's murder. After multiple arrests and releases, a video surfaced showing Vandagriff

and Bryant together. This video, combined with Vandagriff's Twitter post stating that she was happy to get off Tinder and be with a nice man in a bar, gave police the evidence they had been looking for. Charles Bryant was found guilty of murder and dismemberment of Jackie Vandagriff after the jury deliberated for just two hours. By all accounts, Jackie was a dedicated student at the university and friendly to everyone she encountered, making her a possible candidate to haunt TWU.

Unfortunately, in 2019, the university had a well-documented on-campus death, when the body of English professor Dr. Katherine "Katie" McWain was discovered at an undisclosed location on campus. Grief-stricken students and coworkers felt shock and disbelief. A close friend described her as witty, radiant and brilliant. Those closest to McWain knew she suffered from depression, as she had been transparent with this diagnosis. Despite popular opinion, which leaned toward foul play, the medical examiner concluded that McWain died from blunt-force injuries consistent with a self-inflicted fall. Although no formal announcement of a location came from news sources, some state she fell from a window or the roof of the Classroom Faculty Office Building, which stands thirteen stories high. McWain was a dedicated professional who had a passion for teaching and is likely still attempting to teach those willing or able to contact her on campus.

No campus wants students to feel at risk or unsafe, which could be why the news of many tragedies end up buried. It is difficult to prove any story without concrete evidence. It is increasingly difficult to convince smart, educated individuals to believe that stories passed down for generations are false. Did a professor take his own life in Old Main because his desire to dress in a feminine style did not meet the standards of his time? Did a student vanish without a trace from Brackenridge Hall? Could the spirits of these people still haunt the halls? Many chose to believe the stories they heard and the experiences they have on campus.

University of North Texas (Denton County)

Down the street from TWU is another major university that has undergone more name changes and is home to more ghost stories.

On September 16, 1890, Joshua Chilton established Texas Normal College and Teacher Training Institute. Understandably, there was a need for teachers, but the horrendously long names given to universities is still a matter of curiosity. Chilton's goal was to provide advanced education to men and women of Texas. The university first operated from a rental space above a small hardware store in Denton. The first official building was completed in 1891 and was called the Normal Building.

Bruce Hall is the oldest dorm on campus and was built in 1946. *Author's collection.*

In 1901, the state began funding the college, making it a public college, as opposed to a private college. It would undergo six name changes before settling on the University of North Texas (UNT). UNT started as a teacher's college but quickly became known for its diversity and was one of the first colleges to desegregate completely. The concentration on teaching expanded to various other career paths, and the university became known for excellence in musical studies. Famous alumni like Steve Austin, Joe Greene, Don Henley, Meat Loaf, Roy Orbison, Carmen Cusack, Dr. Phil McGraw, Ann Sheridan, Peter Weller, Mike Cochran, Anne Rice and so many others have kept the UNT name known and popular as a substantial university.

A popular figure on campus is a small albino squirrel named Lucky. Not to be confused with Scrappy, the university's eagle mascot, Lucky has become a beloved tradition of luck. Albinism is a genetic condition caused by a recessive gene. In Lucky's case, it means that both his mom and dad carried the gene. Seeing a white squirrel is rare. There are five main places in North America where white squirrels live, and Texas is not on that list. Students believe that seeing Lucky on the day of an exam will bring them

Lucky is an albino squirrel that is thought to bring good luck to students. *Rob Bixby Photography*.

good luck, hence his name and popularity. At this point in the book, I encourage UNT students to block out the next few sentences. While a sighting is rare, there are times when the campus has been without a white squirrel in the mix of many brown squirrels eager to say hello and beg for fresh nuts.

Albino squirrels have been present at UNT since at least the year 2000. At one time, students petitioned to select a second mascot. The first albino squirrel was named Thelonius. His presence led to the establishment of the Albino Squirrel Preservation Society at UNT, which had over four hundred members at one time. Thelonius disappeared in 2003, according to a press release by UNT officials. The second white squirrel was named Baby and appeared around 2004. He lived near the Union, but sadly, a red-tailed hawk swooped down in August 2006 and attacked Baby. Witnesses attempted to stop the attack, but after dropping Baby, the poor squirrel succumbed to his injuries. Thankfully, the perpetrator was not an eagle, the school's mascot. The Willis Library created a memorial to mark Baby's passing. In 2007, a third albino squirrel appeared near Maple Hall, and this one was named Baby's Baby. A professor later reported seeing not one but two white squirrels, leading to the idea that they would mate and produce more squirrels. All was well until a car struck and killed one of the illustrious squirrels in December 2016. This squirrel was preserved via taxidermy and displayed, leaving just one lucky white squirrel on campus. There was a rumored sighting of Lucky in October 2020, but students wonder if this is a ghost or the hidden squirrel. The pandemic stole the beloved lucky charm from UNT. Admittedly, the entry for the name Lucky came from a personal desire to see the mysterious white squirrel scampering across campus.

Some areas on campus have bigger issues than ghost squirrels. Staff members at the student health and wellness center reported ghost activity in their first and second buildings. Many of the employees who worked in the first building brought bricks, equipment and items from the first building to the second building, which could mean they brought the attached spirits.

The University of North Texas opened in 1890 with only seventy students. *Author's collection.*

UNT opened its first library in 1913 as enrollment reached over one thousand students. *Author's collection.*

The original health and wellness center stood between the current health and wellness center and Bruce Hall. The old building was the site of multiple ghost stories and tales of encounters with the paranormal. One late night, after closing, a doctor stayed late to finish his charting. He asked his wife to bring him something from his car. She raced downstairs and back to his office. On the way, she spotted a shadowy figure and called out, "Hello?" The shadow disappeared around a corner without a word.

When she arrived at her husband's office, she asked, "I thought all of the other staff and students were gone?" He informed her that they were indeed alone in the building. She explained her encounter with the shadow figure in the hallway, and the two investigated. No students or staff were found roaming the halls or hiding in the dark rooms of the clinic.

With year-round ghost decorations, laughter comes from my coworkers as they pass my office at the student health and wellness center where I work as a nurse. One coworker said that the resident ghost in the office would appreciate the decorations. The previous occupant of my office collected sock monkeys and placed them on a shelf for decoration. Two workers witnessed small monkeys tossed across the room by an unseen force. Perhaps the monkeys did not approve of her decorations. I have yet to experience any paranormal encounters here.

Students and staff report a sense of someone watching over them when they visit the health center. There are no reports of death in the old or new clinic. UNT police staff often receive reports of a suspicious man with blond hair, torn jeans and no shirt loitering near the health and wellness center. But the suspect is never located.

Bruce Hall is the oldest residence hall at the university. It first opened as an all-female dorm in 1949 and later became a coed dorm. The hall typically houses music majors. Bruce Hall is where Meat Loaf resided during his time at UNT. The hall is said to be haunted by a ghost named Wanda, the spirit of a former student who died in the hall's attic. No specific dates are available, but the historical log states that Bruce Hall housed only females in the earliest years. An unmarried, pregnant woman would not want to draw attention during those years. Wanda is said to have gone to the attic during the last few weeks of her pregnancy to hide her changing body from fellow students. Stories vary depending on who is telling them. They all end with Wanda and her baby dying in the attic at Bruce Hall. Wanda is said to be a friendly spirit but likes to pull pranks like slamming doors and turning the shower off and on. Lacking a specific date or name increased the difficulty of researching Wanda, but a member of the Texas Paranormal Advanced Research team did locate a newspaper article mentioning a female who died of "blood flow" problems in the 1950s. This story matches the account of Wanda giving birth or possibly aborting a child.

The second ghost at Bruce Hall is an elderly elevator repairman. It could be this gentleman who haunts the boiler room by opening the heavy metal doors every time they are closed. An unknown witness has asked the man what he was doing at Bruce Hall, and the man stated he was repairing the elevator. The elevator at Bruce Hall had been nonfunctioning for over thirty years.

Zoe Pratt resided at Bruce Hall and said that living there made her believe in the paranormal. She reported that every time she looked in her mirror, she noticed a strange and obscure figure of a man briefly lingering behind her image. She also said there were times she felt as if someone was getting in or out of her bed. If those events were not enough to scare her, she said that she brought various framed photos to display on her walls. One night, she fell asleep and woke to find all of them off the wall and neatly stacked under a chair in her room. At the time, she had no roommate and no reasonable explanation for the redecoration.

During their investigations, the team caught an EVP on the first floor. The team asked if there was anyone with them and received a faint "yes." They caught multiple other unexplainable, muted voices on their recordings.

The student health and wellness center started as a sanitarium in 1918 and was run under the watchful eye of Nurse Adolphine Grabbe. *Author's collection.*

Phillips said, "It is probably a mixture of real activity along with superstition and college antics."

Former resident advisor Jill Spencer reported that she met a ghost named Brenda in Maple Hall. Wanda seems to have a friend residing in that dorm. Jill admitted to many run-ins with Brenda.

She stated that one of her first encounters took place the week before the student move-in of fall 1995. She and her fellow resident advisors were preparing for the students' arrival. She remembered being up late one night and checking the rooms to ensure they were ready. After checking each room, she turned off the lights and pulled the door closed. A phone started ringing in one of the rooms. Spencer ignored the ring, as this was common when students were gone; it usually meant that a resident forgot to tell friends or family they had moved out. When the ringing continued, Spencer found herself seeking the cause of her annoyance. When she located the phone, she found the room light on and the door open, which was impossible, because she had just taken inventory of that room. As soon as she reached the room, A100, the ringing stopped. Later, when she shared the story, a fellow resident advisor told her about the rumored ghost of room A200.

Showers turn off and on without students being present. Name tags frequently fall from doors. Multiple students report seeing someone walking around the dorm, both inside and out, but they cannot find a living soul when they investigate further.

The moral of these stories is that even if one requests a single dorm room and no roommates, the university cannot guarantee you will not have a nonpaying, invisible guest or roommate.

Sycamore Hall was inspected by a paranormal investigator, Zach Prader, who feels that the building is one of the most haunted sites in the United States, or at the very least the most haunted building at UNT. When his team completed their research, they found that the library was constructed on burial grounds of Romani. Books fall from the shelves, and unexplained voices whisper.

On July 4, 2013, officials found Jonathon Huey asphyxiated on the fifth floor of the general academic building in a computer room where he worked as a student assistant. The twenty-two-year-old had secured the room before hanging himself. Huey's story has brought awareness of the issue of suicide to other students. During National Suicide Awareness Week, officials ask everyone to assist other students in finding the help they need instead of choosing suicide. His death came as a shock to family, friends and fellow students. Friends described Huey as an overall wonderful and kind human being. He was an active cycler and helped at a local bike shop. There are no reports of hauntings in the building, but it would not be surprising to find Huey assisting students in the computer room or maybe creating a gentle breeze as he rides his bike through campus.

The consensus around the campus is that UNT still welcomes a diverse culture and that ghosts are welcome—whether they come in the form of humans or squirrels.

5

SPOTLIGHT SPECTERS

The show must go on, and for some, it never ends. The energy in a theater is phenomenally elevated during rehearsals and performances, contributing to the number of lively spirits floating around theaters worldwide. After all, ghosts require energy to manifest.

In addition, theaters find themselves overpopulated with ghost stories because they are one of the most superstitious locations. Say, "break a leg," and not, "good luck." A bad dress rehearsal means the show will be a success. Leave a seat open for the theater ghost to ensure profitable production. Leave a ghost light on the stage. There is a light, despite the pitch-black darkness of the empty theater. Practicality and safety require some form of light to be cast on a dark stage. A single bulb mounted on a microphone stand or enclosed in a wire cage enables an accessible lighting control console and helps those on stage avoid falling in the dark orchestra pit. These lights are often called equity lights or equity lamps, which indicates that they originated when the Actors' Equity Association mandated them. Theatrical superstition has it that most theaters are haunted by at least one ghost, and many theaters have other superstitions to appease the spirits.

Research into haunted theaters rarely reveals spirits with malicious intent. Those who die in a theater seldom meet their end at the hands of a murderer or in untimely death. Therefore, no remorse lingers in the building or among fellow performers. These ghosts choose to stay within the theater's walls. Some of these ghosts are former theater owners who had a strong passion for the arts and, during their life, may have spent more time and money on the theater than on their home. Many stories tell of an usher who continues working the aisle long after their paychecks stopped. Other theater ghosts are dancers, singers or actors who still thrive in the limelight long after they have passed on. The ghost light allows these spirits to perform on stage and appear to the audience, whether alive or dead.

CAMPUS THEATER (DENTON COUNTY)

ABC Interstate Theaters built the Campus Theater in Denton in 1949 to offer a premier movie theater to the students at the Texas Woman's University and University of North Texas. The venue's style was like that of other theaters of the time. The first movie shown there was *I Was a Male War Bride*, which features former Denton resident Ann Sheridan. The community theater brought residents together to enjoy entertainment for the whole family.

James Parrish Harrison Jr. arrived in Denton in 1938 with the assigned duty of managing three theaters owned by the Interstate Theater Group. While other theaters struggled, Harrison did promotions for vaudeville performances, which helped keep the Campus Theater open. He was the first manager and held that position until 1966, when he retired.

The Campus Theater hosts various talent shows and arts events. *Jonathon Silverberg.*

Harrison dressed in the same sharp gray suit and was known for his great sense of humor, frequently pulling pranks on his employees to keep morale high. He excelled at his job and won two prestigious Quigley Awards in the film industry. He was such a joker that he gave away stray pets as prizes. Patrons and Denton citizens adored Harrison.

Over the years, the theater briefly closed and then reopened as a live performance-arts venue. In 1994, the building underwent a significant renovation, which may have stirred the spirit of the theater manager, who died in 1974.

Visitors hear footsteps in the hallways and often find items relocated without their knowledge. During late-night rehearsals, the lights on the stage flicker on and off. Theater superstition considers it bad luck if the manager does not mess with actors during practice. Manager Harrison pranked the actors when he ran the show. Perhaps Harrison keeps the theater alive and well with his pranks and naughty acts.

In an interview with the local news, Campus Theater volunteer Betsy Deiterman said: "There is a ghost. His name is Mr. Harrison. He was the general manager of the building when it was a movie theater."

Texas Theater (Dallas County)

The Texas Theater opened its doors on April 21, 1931, in the Oak Cliff neighborhood of Dallas. The theater was the brainchild of Oak Cliff resident Clarence "Uncle Mac" McHenry. McHenry partnered to create a solid base for the theater. Harold Robb and Edward Rowley of Robb and Rowley Theater established their name in the business and the Dallas area.

W.G. Underwood popularized drive-in theaters in the Dallas area. David Bernbaum specialized in nickelodeons but also operated theaters. Together, these men had the brains to plot a successful theater.

Architect W. Scott Dunne offered his expertise in creating a Venetian-style theater. The design included opera boxes, huge projectors, a giant chandelier and a state-of-the-art air-conditioning system. The interior design caught visitors' eyes and offered distraction while waiting for the shows to begin.

On November 22, 1963, at approximately 1:45 p.m., the Texas Theater earned a notorious place in world history. But it had nothing to do with the beautiful design, the talented owners or even the show being presented that day.

The exterior of Texas Theater just moments after the assassination of President John F. Kennedy. *National Archives*.

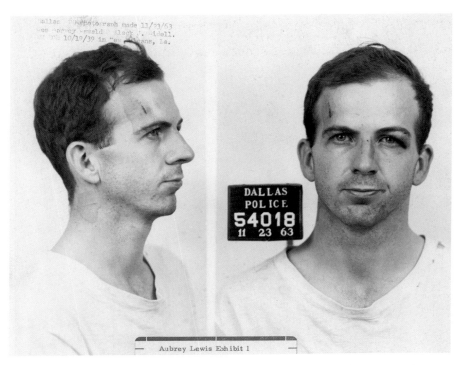

His expression is almost a smirk as Lee Harvey Oswald poses for his infamous mug shot. *National Archives*.

Over fifteen police officers entered the theater, searching for a man who ducked inside while the movie *War Is Hell* played. The man sat in the theater's rear and prayed he had gone unnoticed. Typically, someone sneaking into a theater would not warrant the need for fifteen police officers. In this situation, the officers represented a fellow officer and the president of the United States.

The man who slipped into the theater was Lee Harvey Oswald. He had hid on the sixth floor of the Texas School Book Depository, from where he fired shots into President John F. Kennedy's motorcade. Bullets struck Kennedy and caused fatal damage to his head. Less than an hour after the assassination, Dallas Police officer J.D. Tippit discovered Oswald. Officer Tippit was an eleven-year veteran of the police force and working the beat on November 22 in the Oak Cliff area. Listening to his radio broadcast the assassin's description, Tippit made his way through traffic, searching for the suspect. He pulled his car alongside a man matching the description of the shooter and exited his vehicle to question him. Oswald

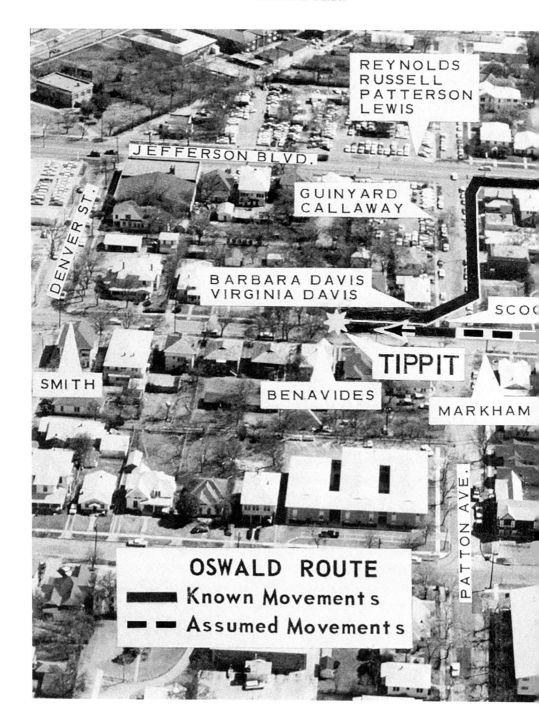

REYNOLDS
RUSSELL
PATTERSON
LEWIS

JEFFERSON BLVD.

DENVER ST.

GUINYARD
CALLAWAY

BARBARA DAVIS
VIRGINIA DAVIS

SCO

TIPPIT

SMITH

BENAVIDES

MARKHAM

PATTON AVE.

OSWALD ROUTE

━━━ Known Movements

┅┅ Assumed Movements

Aerial mapping of eyewitness accounts tracking Lee Harvey Oswald's movements on November 22, 1963. *National Archives*.

drew his handgun and fired three bullets into Tippit's chest and one into his temple. A fifth shot missed entirely. Tippit was pronounced dead fifteen minutes after the shooting. Thankfully, a nearby store manager named John Brewer spotted Oswald slip into the Texas Theater and notified the box office woman, who told police. The theater lights broke the darkness as police entered and found Oswald sitting in the rear. A struggle ensued after Oswald's gun failed to fire. Police removed Oswald from the theater, shouting and screaming.

But it might not be the spirit of Oswald lingering in the theater. Visitors and former employees report seeing shadow figures, hearing whistling in the bathroom and unexplained footsteps, feeling an overall sensation of discomfort and hearing breathing in their ear.

For over two years, Ryan Culbert worked in the theater and had just one paranormal experience. It left a lasting impression and scared him enough for him to pray he did not have a second encounter. "It was in black mist form," he said of the ghost. It was "a figure of a woman in a dress coming down the stairs from the projection room and the safe room stairway as well."

Scott Theater (Tarrant County)

William Scott is known as one of the founding fathers of Tarrant County. He is also known for the majestic theater that bears his name. Scott succumbed to lung cancer before stepping foot in his theater. He had long envisioned creating a beautiful, lush theater in Fort Worth. He left $3 million in a trust fund to develop Fort Worth's cultural district, and the Scott Theater opened its doors in 1966. The five-hundred-seat theater provided space for a variety of cultural and artistic performances. Visitors met with a 575-pound Italian chandelier and a large mural on the wall when entering the building.

Many believe that Scott's passion could be holding him to the theater. After all, he devoted time, energy and a great deal of money. Perhaps he wanted to see the completed project. When the theater opened, some of Scott's paintings were displayed. The vibrations on the building created crooked photos, which did not please Scott. While he is said to haunt the halls and appears walking around and adjusting pictures on the wall, he is not alone.

Many believe the second ghost floating around the Scott Theater is that of a young man named Kenneth Walker Yandal. Yandal was an actor who volunteered at the theater for two years before becoming a salaried employee. Unfortunately, he suffered from depression when his girlfriend broke up with him. The breakup occurred around Christmas or the start of the New Year. Deeply depressed, Yandal hanged himself in the prop room on January 7, 1970.

Laughter heard underneath the stage is believed to be coming from Yandal. His ghost is seen walking across the stage wearing a brown suit. His footsteps go up and down the stairs and across the stage. Items have fallen off the shelves, and power tools have turned themselves on. He shows himself in the basement area near the location of his death.

WRIGHT OPERA HOUSE (DENTON COUNTY)

In September 1894, the Denton County Courthouse found itself a victim of a typical Texas thunderstorm. The damage was too much for the old building, and it was condemned and later demolished. The bricks from the courthouse found a second life when they were repurposed by William Wright, a local rancher who decided to build an opera house. While the opera house faced competition from local moving-picture theaters, it promised to host opera, plays and vaudeville performances. The theater held between seven hundred and eight hundred people.

Although Wright made a profitable earning on his ranch and was known to have one of the largest horse ranches in Texas, he grew bored of ranching. By 1892, he had sold most of his land and ranch. The profit from the sales went into building his mansion, and the rest went to the opera house in Denton Square. He kept only a few pieces of land for his seven children.

Wright passed away in 1906, and with his death, the popularity of the opera house died. Just seven years later, the doors closed. In 1918, it was purchased as a movie theater but never again had the success of Wright's tenure. Different businesses have taken possession of the building, ranging from a department store to an office supply store to a used bookstore.

Wright might respect the current owner, who sells recycled books and records. But there is unrest in the building, and it is hard to determine if it comes from years of remodeling, from the old courthouse bricks or from Wright himself.

There are reports of the ghost of a woman who once lived upstairs in the apartments above the opera house. Named Emma, the ghost is said to float around all three levels of the building and is spotted by visitors. Visitors claim that when they type a search into the computer in the building and hit "enter," the words change to spell "Emma." Perhaps Emma is responsible for the weird noises, unexplained voices and the sense visitors get that someone is standing next to them and breathing down their neck.

As a frequent visitor, I hope to meet Emma or William Wright, but the bookstore gives a calm and comforting feeling. The floors creak and moan, but the rooms contain whispers of customers seeking excitement as they leaf through an old book or discover a vinyl record from the past.

BELAIRE THEATER (TARRANT COUNTY)

A location must be old to be haunted. This belief is a myth, hence this entry for Belaire Theater, which is not even twenty years old at the time of this writing. Copious ghosts haunt the theater, and not all are friendly.

A medium by the name of Cheryl visited the site and said that she felt multiple spirits or at least multiple personalities in the theater. She described them each in detail. She found the first ghost to be playful, vibrant and innocent. This spirit could be the ghost of a young girl whom visitors witness walking in and out of walls. Cheryl described another ghost as sad but good-natured. She felt this spirit belonged to a former employee who loved his job and did not want to leave. A former projectionist died from a heart attack while on the job.

The final ghost Cheryl felt inside the theater was presented as a dark force. Cheryl reported a heavy sensation as if an intense and severe pressure was holding on to her. She described the feeling as "running through water." She also felt a tightening around her throat and declared that this presentation might not be human.

MAJESTIC THEATER (DALLAS COUNTY)

John Eberson designed the Majestic Theater in 1921. Millionaire Karl Hoblitzelle chose Eberson, who was renowned for theater design. Hoblitzelle invested in real estate, owned theaters and was a philanthropist in his spare time. He was the first to add air-conditioning in the theaters and the first in the South to add sound. He had owned and operated a theater of the same name that burned to the ground in 1917. But he was not about to give up on the Majestic Theater. His newest addition to his real estate collection opened its doors on April 11, 1921.

The Majestic became Hoblitzelle's flagship theater, and he ran it with great pride. Some believe he is still overseeing operations inside the venue. Doors open and close of their own accord. Lights flicker off and on. Strange fragrances float through the theater air, and backdrops move independently.

Joy Tipping, a journalist for the *Dallas Morning News*, reported that she worked at the theater in her twenties. Her office always had a chill, and

The Majestic Theater was built in 1920 and, at over one hundred years old, still stands strong. *Highsmith, Mary via Library of Congress.*

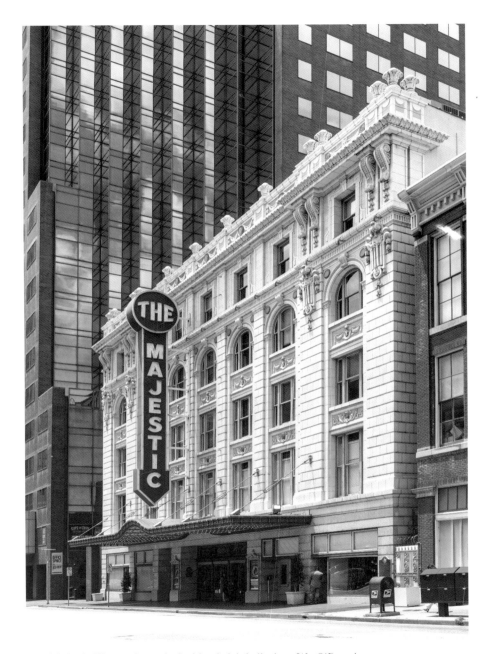

The Majestic Theater is marked with a brightly lit sign. *Wes O'Donnel.*

she frequently wore a sweater to cope with the temperature. Tipping often worried about the security of her office. When she left at night, she triple-checked the locks. Arriving the next day, she found the office unlocked, which was an unusual experience. When she spoke to others about this strange occurrence, she learned that her office had belonged to none other than Hoblitzelle himself. She also learned that he would sneak into the theater at night, and the office door was his entrance to the theater.

6
H$_2$O NO!

Two hydrogen atoms and one oxygen atom combine to form a well-known substance with many mysteries and essential properties. Water is arguably the most essential liquid in the world. All living things—humans, plants and animals—would vanish without water. A familiar theory among paranormal investigators is that water amplifies paranormal activity. Water is an inferior conductor of electricity, so speculations about increased paranormal activity around electrical conductors do not fit the theory. But running or moving water is a different story. Spirits flock to an electromagnetic field, which appears in limestone-rich water and moving water. Of course, water can give life and take life. While the human body is roughly 60 percent water, water in the lungs causes death. Inhaling water whether by accident or with intent, the average adult may drown in as little as one-quarter cup of water if inhaled into the lungs. Water-related deaths are not unusual.

Despite the use of energy to manifest, most water hauntings are residual. The National Paranormal Society defines residual haunting as "an event stuck in an eternity, which gets repeated at times." Investigators often describe this experience as like "watching a movie." While the event repeatedly plays like a skipping vinyl record, these ghosts interact only with the objects known in their memories and their past. They are incapable of communicating or interacting with the living. These repeated playbacks can be auditory, visual or olfactory and are primarily related to a traumatic ending to the spirit's life. Footsteps in the night, a woman walking with a wet dress clinging to her body, a stark scream that pierces the night air and even the pungent odor of a stagnant swamp can present in residual water hauntings.

GOATMAN'S BRIDGE (DENTON COUNTY)

Alton, Texas, was the county seat from 1850 to 1856, but this small town had just a few homes, a blacksmith, three stores, a saloon, a school, two doctors, a hotel and a handful of lawyers. Long after the town died, the King Bridge Company constructed a 145-foot bridge connecting Denton to Cooper Canyon. Built in 1884, the historic iron-truss bridge was known as the "Old Alton Bridge." Motorists signaled prior to crossing by honking their car horns. While an essential connection between cities, the bridge's fame came almost fifty years after its construction.

Based on historical events, the legend of the Goatman starts with Oscar Washburn. An honest and dependable goat farmer, Washburn moved his family north of the bridge. His farm offered meat, milk and cheese, but because of his location, he needed a way to advertise. Washburn placed a sign at the entrance to the bridge to announce that his farm lay ahead. These were normal and acceptable actions. But this was 1938, and the local Ku Klux Klan had labeled Washburn a successful person of color, and they couldn't tolerate his success. They plotted their vengeance.

The historic Alton Bridge features iron trusses and was bult in 1884. *Mark Adkins*.

Right: The tragic death of Oscar Washburn lay the foundation for the legend of the mysterious Goatman. *Mark Adkins*.

Below: The story of a goat herder by the name of Jack Kendell haunts the bridge. Cowboys lynched Kendell and then watched him come back to life as a half man and half goat. *Author's collection*.

A mob went after Washburn by crossing the bridge without headlights in the still of the night. They burst into his home and dragged him to the bridge, where they promptly placed a noose around his neck. They brightened their headlights, placing the execution in the spotlight before tightening the rope and pushing Washburn off the edge. The Klan celebrated their victory as they ran to the bridge's underside to witness Washburn's demise. To their dismay, they found an empty noose and placid water. They searched the area, but it was as if Washburn had vanished into thin air. Infuriated, they ran back to the small cabin housing Washburn's wife and children. Hoping to draw Washburn out of his hiding spot, they filled the air with screams from his family. The stories vary. Some say the small cabin was burned; others say the family died from slaughter. Either way, the Washburn family perished. The tale lived on for many years.

Local college students, professional paranormal investigators and those wanting a night fright seek the bridge in hopes of experiencing signs of the Goatman. Some legends claim that flashing your headlights and knocking on the bridge makes a beast appear—a half goat, half man. Most agree

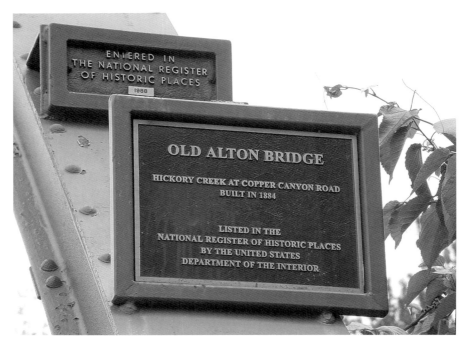

The disappearance of Washburn and voodoo magic performed by Kendell cause many people to feel that this bridge is a portal to another world. *Author's collection.*

that this location holds a residual haunt that replays the unjust killing of an innocent man and his family. Ghostly figures appear in the wooded area, and strange lights flash. Visitors report the feeling of being pushed or touched by an unseen entity.

Ghost Adventure's Zak Bagans filmed an episode at Goatman's Bridge. His crew investigated the Washburn story and tales of a demonic presence. Investigator Aaron Goodman reported a ghost knocking him down during the investigation; Zak felt an overwhelming urge to choke himself. Could this be Washburn trying to demonstrate his manner of death, or is it a dark presence lingering from the many demonic rituals held at the location?

CRAZY WATER (PALO PINTO AND PARKER COUNTIES)

James Lynch left Denison, Texas, with his family and fifty head of cattle headed west, hoping for a drier climate to aid in recovery from malaria. Lynch and his wife also suffered from rheumatism, making travel painful and difficult for the duo. They would not make it far before hearing about Comanche attacks in the West and found themselves settling among the beautiful hills of Palo Pinto County. Lynch found the four-mile journey for water too problematic and decided to drill a well. In the summer of 1880, he traded family oxen for the labor of an experienced well-driller. The water, however, had a strange taste. Lynch allowed the cattle to take the first drinks before subjecting himself or his family to possible further damage due to ingestion. After the water was safely tested, Lynch consumed some and found it rich in healing properties. It did not take long for word to spread, and visitors from all over rushed to try a taste of the miracle water. This popularity led to the creation of Mineral Wells, Texas, and James Lynch named himself the first mayor.

As settlers drilled more wells, they found the area rich in minerals. While modern companies sell vitamin- and mineral-infused water, one Mineral Wells company uses the slogan, "Infused by mother nature. Not some factory." The Crazy Water company relates the story of its beginning, which dates to late 1881, when townsfolk noted that an old lady who had dementia visited the well daily. As time passed, she exhibited marked improvement. It was as if the magical well water cured her dementia.

Ed Dismuke sought help from his doctor to cure his stomach ailments. He failed to find relief until he started drinking water from the Crazy Well.

From the outside, this appears to be an average hotel, but the water from the mineral springs makes this location anything but ordinary. *TexasExplorer98*.

Within a short time, he noted improvement, and by 1904, he had started the Famous Mineral Water Company. His company started bottling and selling mineral-rich water from the well. Dismuke lived to the age of ninety-seven, when he died after falling and breaking his hip. His company is still in business as of 2023. This famous well is located in the basement of the Crazy Water Retirement Hotel.

What is in the paranormal potion that sits under Mineral Wells, waiting for discovery? The name created by the tale of the demented woman is catchy. But the Crazy Water company says that it cannot validate the story of the woman or the possibility of someone being cured by drinking its water. The mineral water contains calcium, magnesium, potassium, bicarbonate (HCO_3), sulfate, zinc, silica and lithium. While the company's water varies in potency, it contains the same minerals.

SCREAMING BRIDGE (TARRANT COUNTY)

The bridge is long gone, but the legend and the haunting screams continue at the location of this North Texas tragedy. Newspaper articles verify the ghastly events, which involve the bridge known to locals as "Death Bridge." It is possible to locate the layout of the former bridge by following the railroad tracks along Greenbelt Road, formerly old Arlington-Bedford Road.

Teenagers and thrill-seekers knew about the rickety old bridge spanning the ravine. The Rock Island Railroad tracks ran parallel, and this combination presented a danger for vehicles, trains and pedestrians. In a time of drag racing and kids proving their courage with risky games of chicken, the bridge broke the boredom. Countless deaths occurred from automobile and train accidents and various mishaps, but the statistics only added to the hype of challenging fate.

The North Texas winter of 1961 proved to be inhospitable. Snow and ice covered the land in a glistening layer of white crystal. January and February marked some of the coldest weather in Dallas history. On February 4, 1961, six teenage females attended a showing of the movie *The Innocents*. The psychological thriller had the girls' adrenaline rushing, and they decided to delay their return home. They ventured toward the death bridge with adventure in mind, but the night took a dark turn. The driver dimmed the headlights and stomped on the accelerator as they approached the bridge. The driver knew she only needed to drive fast and straight. The falling snow covered the flashing headlights on the other side of the bridge. Bill Young heard their car approaching as he sat in his car on the opposite side of the bridge. He honked his horn and flashed his lights but realized that the oncoming driver might not see his warning. The brakes screeched, and the passengers in the car began to scream in terror. Young could do nothing but watch as the car dropped into the desolate thirty-five-foot chasm below.

Just a few days before, a group of four high school boys decided to pull an epic prank. Using a match and a pile of straw, they lit a small fire on the bride and drove away. The fire destroyed the old bridge. No formal charges were given to the boys, as the judge determined they did not intend any harm and held good standing with their Christian school. Warning signs lined the road on both sides of the annihilated bridge, but vandals stole the signs days before the accident involving the girls.

The driver of the car and two passengers died on that cold night in February. The other three passengers suffered severe injuries and required hospitalization. Their screams live on and can be heard by those who visit the area at night. Some suggest it is nothing more than an urban legend and an attempt to maintain the bridge location as a scare tactic. But the fateful night with the teenagers and many other documented stories lean toward this being a location given to hauntings.

McDow's Hole (Erath County)

Just three miles north of Alexander, Texas, is a water hole. Jim McDow owned a large portion of the land in the area. A sustainable town for pioneer settlers required a steady water system. Greens Creek has a bedrock bottom that keeps the water from drying up. A hole was created and a spring fed McDow's land. The spot provided water to both people and livestock over the years. Sadly, the area marks the location of violent events.

McDow's nephew Charlie Papworth purchased a spot of land a few feet from McDow Hole and built a cabin for himself; his wife, Jennifer; and their infant son. They welcomed a second son five years later. Their happiness ended when they heard that Charlie's dad had died about two hundred miles away. Two young children prevented Jenny from traveling with her husband. Instead, she spent her days in and around the cabin tending to the children. After sundown, Charlie insisted his family stay with the McDows or the neighboring Keith family at night. Jennifer packed up the children every evening and did as her husband wished. About a month after Charlie left, the McDow family woke to find that Jenny and the children had not come over the night before. They searched the Papworth cabin, but there was no sign of Jenny or the boys. The tiny house showed signs of a struggle, with overturned chairs and a small spot of red on the floor. A muffled sob led them to the bed, where they found Jennifer's five-year-old son, Temple. He talked but could not give a clear account of the events and did not know his mother's whereabouts. A search party was formed.

A man named W.P. Brownlow pointed to the Comanche tribe, despite reports that there were not many in the area. The search party did not find Comanche or the Papworth family before Charlie's return. Brownlow figured that Charlie would take the law into his own hands and so set a plan in motion. He started spreading rumors about Charlie, saying that he was a horse thief. Brownlow gathered a vigilante group and set out for Charlie's cabin.

Charlie and the other men waited as the executors placed a noose on each man's neck and the men were hanged until their death. Charlie was the last in line to die, and just before they raised his body, Brownlow suggested killing Temple. Little did they know that the old pecan tree was Temple's favorite climbing tree. He made his way up the tree and cut the rope holding Charlie. Charlie survived and fled town with his son the next day, never to return.

Brownlow confessed to killing Jennifer and her baby after Jennifer discovered him rustling cattle. This confession did not help locate their bodies or allow Jennifer to rest. Her ghost travels around the cabin, the creek and the train tracks. She holds her infant in her arms as she wanders the land. Her ghost appears to train engineers, fishermen, neighbors and locals passing by the cabin.

The next person to live in the cabin was Charlie Atchinson. He locked himself inside the place and boarded up the windows and doors as if blocking someone or something from entering. When he disappeared, locals broke into the house to find the man dead. Is it possible that the ghost of the murderer is still haunting the house?

GREEN ELM CEMETERY BRIDGE (JACK COUNTY)

The Green Elm Cemetery is located near the Green Elm Bridge, where the west fork of the Trinity River comes into the northwest of Lake Bridgeport. It was first known as Verner Cemetery, which Harvey Warner first owned and surveyed. When his third wife, Martha, died in 1877, she became the first interment. In an unmarked grave, Verner would join his wife in 1893. The name changed to Green-Wood Cemetery before Green Elm Cemetery was chosen. Currently, the cemetery holds twenty-nine marked graves and is rumored to hold over fifty bodies in all.

Nearly twenty years ago, a ninety-two-year-old man named G.E. Francis retold the tale of his haunting experience at the Green Elm Cemetery Bridge. It was October 1948. After a trip out West to purchase cattle, Francis was one of four cattlemen on their way back to Chico, Texas. The men reached the "Bottoms" area, the old stretch of road between Wizard Wells and Chico. Water covered most of the roadway despite the recent droughts, making travel difficult. They had been driving for several hours in a dark sedan with no air-conditioning. Fatigue set in, and they were in dire need of a bathroom break. The car came to a stop midspan of the Green Elm Cemetery Bridge. Relieved to have a short break and a chance to stretch their legs, the travelers eagerly jumped out of the vehicle. Little did they know, this stop would change them forever, as a bloodcurdling scream unexpectedly filled the air. It came from less than one hundred feet away.

Francis reported, "We saw this thing. It floated in the air about eighteen to twenty feet above the river, and it was moving rapidly toward the bridge."

As the apparition moved closer, the details presented themselves, revealing what appeared to be a Mexican woman wearing a white dress or gown. She thrashed in the water as if drowning until the water carried her away.

A photographer creates a creepy feeling with this snapshot taken in the Green Elm Cemetery. *Nicolas Henderson.*

Francis noted that his fear kept him motionless. He did not know if he should run, hide or jump back in the hot car. She floated over the top of the bridge and moved about five hundred feet south, toward the cemetery. At that point, she vanished as quickly as she had appeared. The men returned to their car and sped away.

Francis recalled, "A fella don't forget that kind of thing. It stays with you always."

Years later, the story leaked out, and the bridge beckoned teenagers and thrill-seekers who hoped to catch a glimpse of the distressed woman.

LAKE TEXOMA GHOST TOWNS (GRAYSON COUNTY)

In 1944, the United States Army Corps of Engineers built the Denison Dam to hold the waters of the Red River. George Moulton had considered building this dam in 1925. He began lobbying his idea in the 1920s, and Sam Rayburn joined him in the 1930s. The two men acted, resulting in the formation of Lake Texoma, the twelfth-largest U.S. Army Corps of Engineers lake in the state.

During World War II, construction and funding came with the Flood Control Act of 1938. The dam was intended to hold floodwaters. German prisoners of war helped in the dam's construction, which was completed in January 1944 at a cost of $54 million. In order to accomplish the goal of freeing the land from flooding, some railroads, highways, utilities, cemeteries, businesses and homes had to be relocated. Four small towns gave up their identity, disappearing under the water.

Located on the Red River, Preston, or Preston Bend, Texas, prospered in the 1800s because of its strategic location. The town was situated in the path of many cattle drives. But as cattle drives diminished, business in Preston died out. After Lake Texoma was created, only the cemetery remained. The cemetery was expanded, and some underwater graves received new homes on dry land.

Hagerman, Texas, was originally named Steedman to honor a Grayson County judge. The town, established in 1880, kept that name until the railroad arrived in 1909. At that time, the name was changed to honor railroad attorney James Hagerman. By the 1930s, even the post office had closed. When Lake Texoma was formed, the town sank to the bottom.

Settlers arrived at Cedar Mills, Texas, in 1870. Grain and lumber mills brought the town to life and attracted local farmers and loggers. The city

The Denison Dam created Lake Texoma and is located between Texas and Oklahoma. *Library of Congress.*

This example of a cotton gin is much like the Henderson Magnus gin that exploded. Such events were not uncommon with this dangerous machinery. *Library of Congress.*

added a racetrack and hotel to attract visitors in 1884. The population grew to almost five hundred, but by 1930, it had dropped to fifty. During a drought in 2011, several tombstones floated to the surface. The desecration of graves added a haunting aspect to its history.

The fourth town to disappear under the lake was Woodville, Oklahoma. Approximately 360 residents lived in Woodville in 1944. Legend has it that Bonnie Parker and Clyde Barrow camped near the town to watch chicken fights.

Paradise Cove is nestled along the lake and continues to haunt locals. In 1899, Dellie Jones visited the Henderson Magnus cotton gin with her younger brother Harrie. She was about sixteen years old, and her brother was six. The siblings stopped to get a drink of water. Unfortunately, their timing was bad. The cotton gin exploded, instantly killing Harrie and one of the gin workers. The explosion took Dellie's legs, and she later succumbed to her injuries. Harrie and Dellie's final resting spot is the Paradise Cove Cemetery. Their graves are among the 2,500 relocated burials. Visitors report rustlings in the woods surrounding the camp and Paradise Cove. There are also reports of a young boy and a girl running from the cemetery toward the camp.

7

BEHIND BARS BOOS

Law and order are essential to forming new towns and cities. The Texas
Constitution derived from six previous versions, and officials adopted
it into law on February 15, 1876. At more than eighty-five thousand
words, it is the second-longest state constitution in the United States. The
territory's extensive history and journey toward independence is the likely
cause for the large word count. Texas also holds the distinction of being the
largest state in the nation.

The creation of the state police took effect under an order from Governor
Edmund Davis on July 22, 1870. At the start, it faced controversy and
adversity. Young cities welcomed the presence of able-bodied officers who
would protect them from hostile Native Americans and outlaws. Governor
Davis controlled the police and supported the employment of African
American officers. In the aftermath of the Civil War, not all citizens felt
that this was feasible or even justifiable. Other turbulence came when the
first police captain, Jack Helm, stood accused of murdering prisoners. In
addition, Chief James Davidson embezzled almost $40,000 before fleeing in
1872. This original iteration of law enforcement ended on April 22, 1873.
The entity re-formed on January 23, 1844, as the Texas Rangers.

Despite the few individuals who chose to corrupt the system, officials
knew that the police force would not survive if they did not enforce laws and
protect citizens. The Wild West gave birth to outlaws, those who lived outside
of or beyond the law. Texas became home to some of the most notorious
criminals and outlaws in North America. Some found themselves behind

bars, while others became statistics in the extreme history of executions. According to multiple sources, Texas has become ground zero for state-sanctioned executions. Three counties account for more than half of the nation's current death row inmates, and those counties are in North Texas. As of the writing of this book, about 1,328 people have died via execution in Texas. These numbers are significant in determining possible haunted locations, because the spontaneous ending of a life via murder, suicide or execution can create unrest or call for the completion of unfinished business.

FORT WORTH ZOO (TARRANT COUNTY)

The Fort Worth Zoo was founded in 1909. When it opened to visitors, one lion, two bear cubs, an alligator, a coyote, a peacock and a few rabbits roamed the sixty-four-acre plot of land. It is the oldest zoo in the state of Texas. While the beginnings were humble, today the zoo has grown into a nationally ranked facility that hosts more than seven thousand native and exotic animals. It is also home to at least two ghosts.

One ghost is a woman in nineteenth-century clothing and holding a parasol. She paces in front of the café. Some people feel that she is waiting for a friend to join her for a meal.

The other ghostly figure comes with a verifiable newspaper story detailing the death of an elephant trainer in 1987. Thirty-five-year-old Michael Bell attempted to move Sam, a four-ton Asian bull elephant, and two female elephants from one pen to another. Sam, who had been in an isolated observation area, attempted to show his dominance to the female elephants. This may be why he was initially separated from the other elephants. As Bell moved the elephants, Sam started acting erratic and used his trunk to grab Bell and throw him to the ground. This action was not normal, as the elephant was familiar with Bell and had never previously acted out. All accounts from those familiar with Bell and Sam claim that the act was most likely unintentional. They believe the elephant was asserting his dominance in front of the female elephants.

Bell lay on the ground as Sam began to stomp on his head. Bell's assistant, John Leggett, rushed to rescue his friend and dragged his lifeless body away from the elephant. Unfortunately, it was too late. Bell succumbed to his injuries. This was the first fatal accident in the seventy-eight-year history of the zoo.

This elephant is not the one mentioned in the story but has resided at the Fort Worth Zoo. *Owen0306.*

Michael Bell might be the second apparition floating around the Fort Worth Zoo. Visitors often see a zookeeper walking near the elephant pen, but the figure is faint and disappears. Bell may continue working his shifts at the zoo, or it could be a residual haunting making an appearance repeatedly.

DENTON COUNTY HISTORIC COURTHOUSE (DENTON COUNTY)

Established by the Texas legislature on April 11, 1846, Denton County came to life just after Texas aborted the dream of being a republic and joined the United States of America. The new county was named for John Denton, a pioneer preacher and lawyer who lost his life during a fight on May 22, 1841. His final resting place is in the center of Denton Square.

Denton was named the official county seat in 1857, when settlers decided that the site needed to be at a central point of the county. A two-story courthouse was built on the north side of the downtown square. But the building and most of its archived county records burned in 1875. A brick courthouse took its place until lightning damaged the building. In 1894, officials condemned and destroyed the courthouse, which included a jail with a holding cell on the bottom floor and gallows just feet away.

Denton County began construction on a new courthouse in 1895. Builders placed the first cornerstone in 1896, and the dedication took place in 1897. The facade symbolizes the unity of Texans from all over the state. The limestone, known for increasing spiritual activity, comes from Denton; the pink granite comes from Austin; the red sandstone is from the Pecos area; and the tan sandstone is from Mineral Wells. The building found its way into the National Register of Historic Places on December 20, 1977, and currently serves as a history museum. Many believe the spirits of John Denton himself and other early settlers linger around and inside the building.

Thomas Murrell lived in Gainesville, Texas, and was an affluent farmer. Before sunrise on April 12, 1894, Murrell began his daily livestock feeding. As he entered the barn, he had no way of knowing that a man sat silently waiting to pounce.

As Murrell exited the barn with his hands in the air, his last words were, "Do not shoot me, Mr. Crews."

John Quincey Adams "Jack" Crews ignored the pleas, and a shot rang out from his weapon. Hearing the shot, Anna Murrell ran out of the house and toward her husband. She knelt on the ground and frantically began delivering aid to her husband as blood seeped from his chest. Another shot filled the air, and Anna collapsed over her husband's body. Crews swiftly took Murrell's watch and emptied the money from his pockets before saddling Murrell's best horse and riding away.

Murrell had recently fired Crews, causing Crews to threaten to kill Murrell's son, Morgan, who worked at a farm down the road. The farmhand hurried to warn Murrell's son of the impending threat. The farmhand arrived a

The Denton County Courthouse is constructed with granite, sandstone and locally quarried limestone, all of which can create spiritual power. *Author's collection*.

Left: The Denton County Courthouse was built in 1896 in the Romanesque revival and Second Empire styles. *Author's collection.*

Below: Standing tall as the centerpiece of the historic Denton County Square, the courthouse appears as a majestic castle. *Texas Historical Commission via National Archives.*

Denton became the county seat, as it sat in the center of the county. *Texas Historical Commission via National Archives.*

few moments too late. Thankfully, the son lived long enough to explain the incident to the farmhand. The farmhand witnessed Crews shoot Morgan Murrell dead as he was plowing the field. Crews chased Murrell's other son, Leonard, into a farmhouse but could not find him. Crews fled the crime scene on his stolen horse in a fit of anger.

Sheriff Pat Ware formed a posse, which started with only forty men and increased to almost five hundred before the search ended. Ware arrested Crews, but taking him safely to jail proved difficult, as over two hundred farmers were seeking vengeance for Thomas Murrell and his family. A mistrial was declared in Crews's first trial, bringing a second trial to Denton. Crews was convicted and sentenced to hang on October 14, 1895.

Officials erected the gallows on the north side of the jail, and a coffin sat under the gallows. When Crews spotted one of Murrell's sons in the audience, he stopped his speech and shouted out, "Howdy, Mr. Murrell."

This hanging would go down in history as the last execution in Denton County. According to the local newspaper, over 10,000 people attended the public hanging. (The entire population of Denton was closer to 3,500 at the time of Crew's execution.) The execution took place a few blocks from the courthouse, and Crews might still be roaming the site of his final departure.

There are reports of shadow figures in the windows when the building is closed to the public. Several visitors have reported seeing a man in a cowboy hat looking down.

WISE COUNTY COURTHOUSE (WISE COUNTY)

The common phrase "the third time is a charm" was insufficient for Wise County. The county went through courthouses quicker than it could build them and required three previous attempts before its current courthouse reached completion.

The first courthouse came to life in 1858 after the conversion of a sixteen-square-foot frontier trading post made of hackberry wood. County officials were more concerned about having a courthouse than its size or construction. By 1861, officials knew they needed a more significant courthouse to accommodate the growing county. The new structure was a two-story, forty-by-forty-foot wooden building in the Greek Revival style. Fire destroyed this second courthouse on November 26, 1881. Reports indicate that an arsonist started the fire, but no one was charged for the crime. This fire led to the third Wise County Courthouse, erected in 1883. A fire consumed the building just two years later, on January 12, 1895. Unfortunately, county officials did not learn their lesson about fire prevention. Their only innovation was hiring an employee to stand guard and grab all court records in the event of a fire.

The beige exterior of the Wise County Courthouse resembles a castle, with peaks and turrets adorning the sides. *Billy Hathrone.*

In 1896, the county constructed the fourth and final courthouse in the middle of the town square. Many believed it was far too extravagant and costly. But this time, it was constructed from precut stones that would stand their ground in the case of another fire. It is the oldest operating courthouse in the state of Texas.

On February 23, 1897, Jailer Floyd Coberly went to work at the Denton County Jail. It was only his tenth day on the job. Eighteen-year-old George Henry and two other men faced burglary charges and were being held in the jail. After lunch, Jailer Colberly was making his rounds when Henry delivered several blows to the jailer's head with a blunt object. One blow to the back of his head proved fatal. As Coberly fell down the stairs, Henry ran after him to get the jailer's gun. But another inmate stopped the confrontation. Henry instead decided to flee the scene. He first unlocked all the cell doors, then escaped with his accomplices. Police apprehended Henry on the edge of town, and Wise County tried him for the murder of Coberly. George Henry received a sentence of execution by hanging at the gallows just outside the Wise County Courthouse. He was hanged on February 18, 1898, almost one year after his crime.

The frequent fires and one-time execution may or may not cause the strange happenings at the courthouse. Visitors hear and see the courtroom door slam when no one is near it. Visitors also report that the elevator goes up and down independently and without visible occupants.

OLD RED DALLAS (DALLAS COUNTY)

By 1890, Dallas County's population had grown to nearly triple its original size. The need for law and order became essential, and the current accommodations were not extensive enough to handle the large population. Often referred to as "Old Red," the former Dallas County Courthouse was constructed in 1892. The Romanesque structure was built with red sandstone and accented in marble. Historical archives are unclear if this is the fourth, fifth or sixth courthouse for Dallas County, but most historians agree that it is likely the sixth. The first was a ten-by-ten-foot log cabin belonging to John Neely Bryan, one of Dallas's founding fathers, and it functioned from 1846 to 1848. A second courthouse, only slightly larger than the first, was constructed in 1850 out of wood planks and had a mud chimney. The third courthouse came in 1855, and contractors used brick construction this time. The two-story building remained the courthouse for nearly seventeen years. In 1872, a sandstone structure with a fancy dome became the fourth courthouse, but it burned down in 1880. The fifth courthouse served for just nine years before burning down, making way for "Old Red," which continued in use until the 1990s.

A few people died on or near the property. There are discrepancies as to the exact location of the hanging that served as the first known legal execution in the state of Texas. It occurred in the courthouse jail yard on May 17, 1853.

Edward Welborn sold an enslaved African American named Jane to a man by the name of John Young in 1844. Jane was sold again, to a man named Smith Elkins. Elkins's wife sent Jane to work for Andrew Wisdom in 1853. Wisdom was a widower with two small children and needed help raising the children and keeping his house in order. Questions remain over events that took place involving Wisdom and Jane. Jane faced murder charges in Wisdom's death, and Wisdom's children became orphans as the result of a few swings of an axe blade.

Trial notes indicate that Wisdom was asleep when Jane split his head with an axe. In court, Jane stated, "Yes, and I'd do it again."

The Dallas County Courthouse is constructed from red sandstone with rusticated marble accents. It is referred to as "Old Red." *National Archives.*

Old vehicles travel down Elm Street in Dallas's city center. *Author's collection.*

July 1, 1881, Adam Thompson was hanged for robbery and murder.

July 28, 1893, Henry Miller was hanged on the stairs of the jail for murdering a police officer.

On September 2, 1898, Joseph Malone faced execution by hanging on the stairs of the jail for rape and attempted murder.

Holly Vann was convicted of robbery and murder and was hanged on May 12, 1905.

February 1910, police found a sixty-five-year-old man named Allen Brooks in the loft of his employer's home with the employer's three-year-old daughter. The child had been missing for four hours before police located them. Investigation determined that Brooks had raped the child. Charged with the crime, Brooks was taken into custody to await trial. But community outrage put pressure on vigilantes to act.

On March 3, 1910, a mob pushed Brooks out the courthouse window and dragged him down the street. An angry mob tied a rope around his neck and he was dragged for nearly a mile. The mob then stomped on his head. A mob lynched Brooks while over five thousand people watched. Children ripped pieces of Brook's clothing to keep as souvenirs.

The construction of Old Red began in 1890 and was completed in 1892. *National Archives.*

The Dallas County Courthouse includes columns of local granite and turrets that stretch almost 120 feet into the sky. *National Archives.*

Julius Robertson was hanged for murder on May 13, 1910, and John Robertson was hanged for murder, assault and robbery on January 10, 1913.

The county hanged Floyd Stanton on August 1, 1913, for murder.

The county hanged Ed Long on December 19, 1913, for the murder of an officer.

Walter Stevenson and Leonard Dodd died by hanging on May 24, 1918, for kidnapping and criminal assault. The execution of these two men drew a crowd of over 1,500 spectators.

Officials executed Will Jones for rape and murder on July 22, 1918, and Green Hunter was executed on July 9, 1920, for criminal assault and robbery.

Fred Douglas, also called "Jobo," was the last person hanged in Dallas County, on August 27, 1920. In 1923, Texas legislation called for all legal executions to take place at the state prison in Huntsville.

It is easy to believe that spirits would linger around the old, red courthouse with so much death and despair. Today, the location functions as a museum and contains many historic objects, and this may be the reason for some of the paranormal activities reported by visitors. Many believe a tall, dark shadow figure haunts the site. Considering the death toll within the walls of Old Red, it is no wonder the ghost stories exist.

COLLIN COUNTY "THE PRISON" (COLLIN COUNTY)

The old Collin County Prison is one of the oldest jails in Texas, and to a great extent it remains in its original condition. Contractors completed construction in 1880 using rough-cut blocks of fossilized limestone. Written in stone above the only door in and out are the words, "Collin County Prison."

The jail housed about fifty prisoners and a live-in jailer. Claude West was the son of the Collin County sheriff and became the jailer at the prison. His wife took care of cooking and laundry. Among the more notorious inmates was Frank James, perhaps the prison's most infamous "guest." Ray Hamilton of Clyde Barrow's gang spent time under the supervision of West. Charles "Tex" Watson, a member of Charles Manson's family, had a brief stay here while awaiting extradition to California for his part in the Tate and LaBianca killings.

Stephen Ballew was the first person legally hanged in Collin County. His execution occurred in front of a large crowd on May 24, 1872. Ballew had traveled to the county with a man named James Golden to sell mules. He oozed charm. People freely gave in to Ballew, whether saying "yes" to a marriage proposal or offering $5,000 to invest. Ballew decided to kill Golden just a few miles outside of McKinney. Ballew shot Golden in the back of the head before bludgeoning him with an axe. After burying Golden in a shallow grave, Ballew moved to Collin County to complete his business.

He wrote to the Golden family with a revised version of the events. He stated that it was Golden who betrayed him and then disappeared. The Golden family welcomed Ballew when he returned and even offered him a farm.

Before long, the Golden family started piecing together the puzzle. The family received answers when officials located a body. Ballew could not hear James Golden's name without shivering. He also wore a shirt belonging to James. Ballew was taken into custody.

Reports state that on the day of his execution, Ballew ate a hearty breakfast before leaving the jail and getting in the wagon that carried his coffin. He rode to the gallows smoking a cigar, dressed in a nice suit and wearing a big white hat and dress shoes. The only person in the crowd mourning Ballew was his new wife, Clara.

Ballew's last request was, "Here, Captain, lay my hat over there," as he handed the hat to the sheriff.

In 1882, ten years after Ballew's execution, Sherriff William Warden arrested Shack Culwell for murder. The sheriff later retold the events

Though it sits abandoned, the exterior of this building invites ghosts to come inside and wander the halls. *Tiny Dragons*.

leading up to Culwell's arrest. Court documents revealed that eighteen-year-old Culwell worked for a man named W.R. Norvell. Norvell and his wife were separated, but the children remained with their mother and were present when W.R. was murdered. Culwell claimed that he was owed $3.10 for the work he had completed for Mr. Norvell, and he went to his home to ask for payment. The disagreement became a dispute, and without warning, Culwell shot and killed Norvell in the doorway of his home before fleeing the scene. After a two-week hunt, Culwell was located and arrested for murder. His execution took place on August 18, 1882.

A farmer found the body of a missing man named Hardy Mills. He had been tied up and weighted down before being shoved into a well and left to die. Mills had been missing for fourteen days before his body was discovered. Mills had worked on the Stepp farm, and within an hour of the body's discovery, Ezell Stepp was taken into custody. When the case came to trial, Ezell faced murder charges. Arlie was an accessory to the crime and charged with the murder of Hardy Mills.

After only three hours of deliberation, the jury decided for conviction. Ezell Stepp was found guilty of murder and sentenced to "hang by the neck until dead."

On November 17, 1922, William "Ezell" Stepp was the third and last man legally executed in Collin County. His last words were: "I am innocent. The hanging is unjust. Please do not choke me."

The prison closed for the new facility in 1979. Visitors to the abandoned site describe it as "creepy." On dark and stormy nights, much like the fateful night of Ezell's death, a ghostly figure can be seen hanging in the courtyard of the old prison. Footsteps are heard in the hallways when no people can be seen walking. The building has seen multiple uses over the years, ranging from two different restaurants to a children's bookstore, an art gallery and even an accounting firm. The legend of Ezell Stepp is so strong that those who worked in the building used window coverings to block out any potential sightings of him.

8
TOWERS OF TERROR

The Lenape, or Delaware, are Indigenous people of the northeastern woodlands. By the 1860s, most Native American men and women had been relocated from the Northeast to Oklahoma and settled on reservations designated for their tribes. Many had migrated to Texas by the late eighteenth and early nineteenth centuries. The Lenape remained friendly long after Texas won its independence from Mexico. Republic of Texas president Sam Houston agreed to peaceful relations with the tribes and sought the services of many Native Americans to help protect Texas from hostile tribes. He also fought for land rights for the Lenape, but the next president opposed this action. President Mirabeau Lamar opposed the Lenape and considered them illegal intruders on the settlers' land. He ordered their removal from Texas. Thankfully, in 1842, Houston was reelected. He reinstated his policies with the Lenape, which later proved to be a good move. The Lenape contributed to Texas' history and success as a state.

A Lenape guide and rancher named Black Beaver combined efforts with Jesse Chisholm, who made his living as a merchant. The two assembled cattle and orchestrated drives from Texas to Kansas, where cattle were shipped east for a highly profitable margin. Historians agree that the Chisholm Trail departed at Donna or San Antonio in southern Texas, then traveled through North Texas and ended in Abilene, Kansas.

Hell's Half Acre, in Fort Worth, made for a good resting point, with a stockyard and houses of gambling and prostitution. The hardworking cowboys needed a place to rest at night, as did travelers to all cities in North Texas. Hotels and inns provided shelter and privacy. The four walls of relatively light wood or brick hid outlaws and criminal actions from the eyes of Texas Rangers. Death occurs in temporary accommodations. It was not and still is not uncommon to find a tortured soul lingering in the hallways of hotels and motels.

BAKER HOTEL (PALO PINTO COUNTY)

In 1922, the citizens of Mineral Wells saw a trend of nonresidents profiting from the valuable water held in the many wells. Visitors needed a place to stay, and the town needed a way to keep their profits. Local shareholders generated over $150,000 in funding and secured the help of prominent hotel magnate Theodore Brasher Baker.

Construction began in 1926 with a design that made the Baker Hotel a highlight of Mineral Wells. An Olympic-sized swimming pool held gallons of mineral-rich healing water straight from the city wells deep inside the hotel. It would be the first of its kind. The hotel was unrivaled, with fourteen floors, 450 guest rooms, 2 ballrooms, a beauty salon, a bowling alley, a gymnasium and an indoor pool. The final cost exceeded $1 million, and the structure required three years to complete.

Over the years, prominent and well-known celebrities visited the hotel and soaked in the pool. Lawrence Welk, Clark Gable, Lyndon B. Johnson, Clyde Barrow and Bonnie Parker visited the hotel before its decline. As scientists developed antibiotics and modern medicine advanced, the mineral wells became less popular. By the Great Depression, Baker had declared bankruptcy and gave his nephew Earl control of the hotel management. The hotel experienced ups and downs, and by 1963, Earl declared the doors officially closed to the public. But private investors reopened the doors in 1965 and leased the building from the Baker family until Earl passed away in 1967. At this point, Earl became possible ghost number one. He was living in the hotel's Presidential Suite when he suffered a fatal heart attack at age seventy-four. Workers found him unconscious on the floor. Most paranormal activity surrounding Baker suggests a residual haunt or the possibility of his soul never having clocked out at the end of his shift. He continues to monitor the activities in the building.

In 1972, the massive Baker Hotel was abandoned. In 2019, renovation began to reopen the hotel. *R. Gene Brooks via National Archives.*

The Baker Hotel featured fourteen floors, 450 guest rooms, 2 ballrooms, a beauty salon, a bowling alley and an indoor swimming pool. *R. Gene Brooks via National Archives.*

Construction and renovation, two factors that awakened the restless ghosts, began. From 1974 until 2019, the building remained closed to the public and silent. The COVID-19 pandemic slowed restoration, but in 2021, life at the hotel resumed.

Visitors believe that five ghosts haunt the Baker Hotel. The first is Earl Baker, the workaholic manager. The next is Theodore Baker, who invested his time and money in the hotel and continued to give until he had no money to his name. He may be still roaming the halls to visit his nephew or manage his most lavish hotel. Ghost number three is an unknown prostitute whom workers found dead in one of the rooms. This story comes from generations of tales and is difficult to verify due to the nature of the woman's employment. Another mysterious woman floats around the seventh floor. She is known as the "Lady in White," as guests have seen her in a long, white gown as she glides just inches above the carpeted floors. Some believe this is Virginia Brown. This mistress had a suite on the seventh floor and frequently visited Earl Baker in his Presidential Suite.

The fifth ghost has the most wicked backstory. On January 16, 1948, a fifteen-year-old passenger-elevator operator at the Baker Hotel, Douglas

The Baker Hotel was featured on the television show *Ghost Adventures*. *R. Gene Brooks via National Archives.*

Moore, prepared for work. When he arrived early for his shift, he went to the hotel's bottom floor to visit with friends and coworkers. For the most part, he offered up laughs while the friends awaited their shifts. But one fateful jump left both Moore and his friends in silence. Young Moore jumped in and out of the service elevator while it was in motion. He misjudged the distance and speed, and his body was only partially inside the elevator carriage. His friends jumped into action and desperately tugged at his legs. It was too late. They stood helpless as they watched the elevator continue to rise toward the second floor, crushing Moore's body at his abdomen. Workers struggled to pull his tattered body from the elevator shaft for over thirty minutes. Years later, hotel visitors reported spotting the upper body of a young man leisurely waking around the hotel and feeling cold rushes of air.

Renovation and construction influence the livelihood of a building's spirits. When the Baker Hotel makes its grand reopening, visitors will be able to admire the refurbished classic and know they are in good hands if they stay in the Presidential Suite or take an elevator from the lobby to their floor.

ROGERS HOTEL (ELLIS COUNTY)

Emory and Nancy Rogers stumbled upon Waxahachie, Texas, in 1844. A simple tent marked their first home, and eventually, the couple constructed a cabin. Neither Emory nor Nancy required a lavish home or fancy items. They welcomed travelers into their tiny cabin, and it served as a place for local religious meetings and town meetings. The first election for the county seat took place in the Rogers cabin, and the town won the bid.

Emory and Nancy added a second story to the cabin before the Civil War for additional space to host overnight travelers. In 1870, John Siddons purchased the two-story cabin. He operated the building as Rogers Hotel and changed the name to Siddons Hotel in 1877. In 1881, he sold the building to a realtor, who drew up plans for a three-story hotel with the help of a local architect. The first tragedy struck the hotel just prior to the construction of the new building. On May 9, 1882, the old two-story cabin burned. The original Rogers cabin became nothing more than a pile of blackened soot.

By June 1882, a new brick, three-story hotel had come to life. To honor the original town founder, the hotel operated as Rogers Hotel. This tribute showed residents' desire to build the town and encourage overnight travelers to stop and stay a spell. But on November 12, 1911, the air filled with smoke, and fire destroyed the interior of the building.

The current building stands four stories tall and opened in 1913. Talk about perseverance. The Rogers Hotel operated until 1964, when it was sold. The doors remained closed for over forty years before restoration turned the former hotel into studio apartments. The history of the building and the tragic fires, combined with the recent remodel, contributed to the ghost stories that floated around the building.

On one occasion, the owner showed up in the morning to find the maintenance person locked in his room and trembling with fear. He reported that a man dressed in full Wild West attire approached him. The man asked him to follow him to the basement level, which once held a swimming pool. The stranger pointed to the area where the pool formerly stood and said, "Very bad things have happened here." Before the maintenance man could ask for further details, the man vanished. Stories from the hotel's history include a young girl drowning in the pool.

When interviewed in 2018, one apartment resident stated that she was one of the few residents who had not moved out quickly. She felt at ease in the building but admitted to witnessing strange encounters. After moving into her loft, she noticed a door handle moving on its own. On another occasion, she noted a light flickering off and on, but she blamed this on old electrical wiring.

The ghost stories primarily involve the young girl and the cowboy. Both are signs of ghosts trying to manifest via external energy. Door handles jiggle. The elevator travels to various floors independently, and lights flash off and on. Paranormal investigators experience battery drains and equipment failure. It could be the spirits of one of the more famous visitors who stayed at the Rogers Hotel. Frank Sinatra and the entire White Sox baseball team stayed here.

Despite numerous reports, the spirits at the Rogers Hotel welcome visitors in a fashion that would get Emory and Nancy's seal of approval.

DENISON HOTEL (GRAYSON COUNTY)

In the early 1800s, Denison, Texas, did not have proper overnight housing. In 1890, the National Commercial College built a business college from grand red bricks. Four of Denison's most prominent residents became officers of the college. Around the turn of the century, the Denison Hotel occupied the site. The daily rates ranged from $2.30 to $3.50 and included an electric elevator, private bathrooms, steam heat, phones in all rooms, a barbershop, a billiard parlor and a dining room. The building housed Carter's Music Store and Pace's Furniture Store on the first floor.

The old brick building of the Denison Hotel has undergone renovations but remains the same on the exterior as it did when it was first constructed. *Michael Barberea.*

Manager M.L. Oglesby boasted: "There is no hotel in the Southwest which stands higher with the traveling public than The Denison. It also may be said that no hotel in the entire country offers such superior service on the same modest scale expenditure." Business boomed until January 24, 1920, when the hotel was engulfed in flames for four days and four nights. Over three thousand feet of hose and six streams of water were needed to combat the flames. A handful of employees and guests found themselves trapped in the building. Fire destroyed the majestic hotel and left behind soot and fallen material.

It was not until 1923 that two businessmen, Arthur Simpson and Joe Crumpton, planned a new hotel. Crumpton had led the hotel industry in Denison for many years. He left home as a teenager, during which time he performed in a circus and sowed his wild oats. He settled down in Denison and married Lucy Simpson, the daughter of one of Denison's founders, Williamson Simpson. Lucy's brother Arthur was a businessman who ran various hotels in Texas. Her oldest brother, William, was a millionaire bachelor. Crumpton owned the Place Hotel and partnered with the Simpson brothers to open the Simpson Hotel, which later became the Denison Hotel. Townspeople came for the grand opening on October 1, 1924.

Simpson Hotel, a Victorian-style venue, boomed with business by the early 1920s. Guests entered the hotel lobby and could visit the lounge and dining room, with a grand staircase on the first floor. The second floor featured a smoking room and a small library. The next eight floors housed elegant rooms and a penthouse on the roof overlooking the city. Magician Harry Houdini said, "Nowhere in my travels have I found any better equipped and with better accommodations."

Like a magic trick gone horribly wrong, a fire struck the hotel a second time.

In 1927, a family of four came through Denison, traveling from Texas to New York. A husband and wife and their teenage son and daughter planned to stay at the Denison Hotel for three weeks. A hotel maid was cleaning the room while the family dressed for dinner. A fire broke out in the room above them, but no alarms sounded. The ceiling collapsed, killing the family and the maid. It crashed to a dining room filled with patrons as the fire continued.

A paranormal investigator entered the hotel with zero knowledge of its history. Entering a location having done no research is common practice among distinguished investigators, as this aids in invalidating their findings by preventing falsification or seeing what everyone else saw in a haunted location. The investigator reported that the trouble started when he arrived at the hotel. He was wandering through the halls when he saw a couple of people running down the hallway. When he moved closer to investigate, they disappeared. He also reported hearing strange noises, including footsteps and pounding on the wall. This investigator is not alone in his discoveries, as visitors to the Denison Hotel have reported strange noises and sights while attempting an overnight stay.

Adolphus Hotel (Dallas County)

Adolphus Busch emigrated from Germany in 1857 and married Lilly Anheuser, the daughter of Eberhard Anheuser, in 1861. Busch bought into his father-in-law's brewing company and became one of the first American brewers to use pasteurization to keep beer fresh. He was also the first to use refrigerated railroad cars, which he introduced in 1876. Anheuser's brewing company changed its name to Anheuser-Busch Brewing Association in 1879, and when Anheuser died in 1880, Busch took over the entire ownership of the company.

The Adolphus Hotel was opened in 1912 by the founder of the Anheuser-Busch company. *Daniel Hardy via National Archives.*

A wealthy man, Busch looked to real estate to continue his growth. He planned to build a posh and grand hotel in downtown Dallas. Built in 1911, the Adolphus Hotel opened its doors to the public in October 1912. It was fashioned after a German castle, only much taller. The twenty-two-story hotel was the state's tallest building for over a decade.

The Adolphus is a hotbed for paranormal events and unsettling happenings. It is also one of the top ten haunted locations in the United States. Perhaps the October opening foreshadowed the site as a stomping ground for ghosts and haunted adventures.

Anyone with a fear of elevators might opt for the stairs while staying at the Adolphus. Reports of the elevator doors opening and closing at random times and the elevator car making mysterious stops at all floors might be related to the dark history of these machines. It is not uncommon to see transparent guests in the elevator car, and they all have the same warning: "watch your step."

Prior to the hotel's opening, the Adolphus elevators claimed their first victim. A forty-five-year-old man named Charles McIntosh found himself trapped between the cage and the side of the shaft. While he initially

The Adolphus stands twenty-two stories tall and was once the tallest building in Texas. *Daniel Hardy via National Archives.*

survived this horrendous dragging incident, he succumbed to his injuries a few hours later.

On October 20, 1912, tragedy struck just two weeks after the hotel opened. An Italian waiter named G. Comiro traveled to the third floor to complete his duties. He stood by the elevator entrance and chatted with a coworker as they waited for the service elevator to arrive. A passerby caught Comiro's attention, and he turned away from the elevator. When the elevator door popped open, Comiro stepped backward into the carriage. But the elevator kept moving upward, and Comiro fell three stories down the elevator shaft, landing in the basement. The impact horribly crushed his skull, and although medics took him to the hospital, he died just two hours after his fall.

In 1917, R.A. Fore, an employee of Otis Elevator Company, fell to his death while working on the elevator in the new annex of the Adolphus Hotel. He was on a hoist when he fell to the basement, crushing his skull. There were no witnesses to this fall.

The elevators would see another death in 1917: sixteen-year-old James Muse Jr. Muse went to work as an elevator boy on December 26, 1917,

The Adolphus is still a luxury hotel, but there have been multiple elevator mishaps over the years. *Daniel Hardy via National Archives.*

expecting a typical day's work. The elevator arrived at the sixth floor, where Muse waited. He attempted to enter while the elevator moved, but the doors did not properly close. Stepping into an open elevator shaft, Muse fell from the sixth floor to the basement. His skull was shattered, and both of his legs were broken.

In 1924, thirty-two-year-old Betasar Calvillo was working as a cook at the Adolphus. The elevator operator reported that Calvillo opened the elevator door and looked up to the car to check why it was taking so long to arrive. When the operator was able to identify Calvillo, it was too late to stop the heavy car from striking him. Calvillo died instantly.

On March 15, 1971, porter Ralph Radley Jr. was assisting a band load their equipment onto the elevator. The hotel was a hot spot for bands to perform, and this popular local band waited for the elevator to help move their heavy equipment. They noted an issue with the elevator and, when the doors opened, found themselves staring at an open shaft. The band members warned Radley to double-check if the car was present. After five deaths, this relentless elevator continued to take lives.

The Adolphus has been host to several dignitaries and celebrities. *National Archives.*

Radley checked and called out, "Yes, it is here," before stepping into the empty elevator shaft and falling to the basement below.

Other deaths occurred at the Adolphus. In 1913, an insurance salesman suddenly became ill and dropped to the sidewalk in front of the Adolphus. Onlookers brought the man into the hotel's lobby to tend to his medical needs. Thirty minutes later, the man died. His cause of death was noted as "acute attack of indigestion and apoplexy."

In 1915, an Iowa Cement Company employee drank a bottle labeled "poison." Hotel employees found the bottle next to his lifeless body when cleaning his room.

Rumored deaths resulting in haunts include a jilted bride who hanged herself in the ballroom after her fiancé failed to attend the wedding. She appears roaming the halls in a white, flowing gown. Another ghostly legend states that one of the hotel managers kept a mistress. One night, she was sneaking through the hotel and fell to her death in a hidden passageway.

THE GLEN HOTEL (SOMERVELL COUNTY)

In 1928, Glen Rose, Texas, welcomed a new hotel, The Glen. Nestled alongside the Paluxy River, it provided housing for women awaiting the return of their soldier husbands during World War II. While newspapers did not report every shootout, bullet holes have left their marks on the lobby walls of The Glen. This sordid past might contribute to the copious ghost stories that haunt the grounds.

The scent of cigar smoke, despite the no-smoking policy, has filled the lobby at times. Bright lights materialize and vanish in an instant. Visitors witness shadowy figures floating down the hallway and entering through the closed door of room 9. Guests in rooms 12, 18 and 29 have reported their toiletries being moved and disembodied voices filling the silence. A male presence makes itself known, and women's laughter fills the hotel.

Room 19 is notoriously the most haunted. One witness reported feeling extremely cold when they first entered the room. Later in the night, they felt as if someone was touching their back and as if they were not alone in the room. Could this be the ghost of one of the many women waiting for their husbands to return? This witness also reported feeling breath on his ear before he grabbed a lighter from the nightstand to illuminate the room and see the intruder. He claims that an older woman stared back at him. The

The three-story hotel still receives guests, both living and deceased. *TexasExplorer98.*

woman disappeared when he turned on the bedside lamp to shine additional light on the situation. He was able to calm his nerves until the pungent odor of perfume flooded the room. Female visitors in room 19 sense a familiar male figure but feel eerie as he enjoys watching over them as they sleep. Male visitors sense a female in old-fashioned attire lingering at the foot of the bed or gently touching them as they lay still.

While every room, including the lobby, contains paranormal activities, the ghosts are friendly yet sometimes mischievous.

9

GRAVEYARD GHOSTS

Before 1830, American municipal cemeteries did not exist. Instead, people buried their dead on their property, in a churchyard or in a town's common area. Bodies were often buried alongside a trail as families traveled from city to city. When cemeteries were established, they were, in fact, for the living. Public parks did not exist, but rural cemeteries suited the need perfectly. Families visited their deceased loved ones and shared a meal in the peaceful and quiet surroundings. Large areas of ground filled with beautiful sculptures and flowers made a perfect picnic location. They were called memorial parks, and the term *cemetery* arrived sometime later.

Why would a cemetery have ghosts? A lost soul might not know how to find his old home, but if he waits long enough, those who loved him will visit his grave and provide a chance to see them again. The Dallas–Fort Worth National Cemetery holds more than 76,000 graves over 638 acres. Without a doubt, several of those graves contain spirits that met an untimely death and still have unfinished business here in Texas. Bonnie Parker and Clyde Barrow certainly live it up at the Crown Hill Memorial Park in Dallas. At the very least, they are sneaking into bank vaults at night or meeting up for a midnight stroll through the moonlit cemetery.

LOST CEMETERY OF INFANTS (TARRANT COUNTY)

In the 1800s, unwed mothers faced harsh criticism. And it was not uncommon to become an unwed mother. A woman might lose her spouse, a runaway could have found herself in the wrong place or a young girl might have made one wrong choice. Women who found themselves in any of these precarious positions had limited resources and options. Their own families often shunned them, and society made it impossible for them to work to support their children. Some of these women chose to end their lives. Fortunately for some of these women living near Arlington, Texas, they had another alternative.

Reverend James Upchurch and his wife, Maggie, operated the Berachah Industrial Home. This home sat hidden on forty acres of land and featured a self-sufficient village. The village offered redemption and protection for "erring girls," or girls who failed to adhere to the proper and accepted standard.

Acceptance into the home meant that each female had to work and do chores. They received training as a seamstress, printer, typesetter or laundress. The management mandated church services for everyone who lived in the home. The final stipulation was that each woman needed to prove that they could support and care for their child for one year. Failure to do so meant that the baby went up for adoption.

Left: The cemetery holds over eighty graves marked with first names or simply the word *baby*. *Author's collection*.

Right: In the late 1800s, unwed or widowed mothers hid or were hidden from the public eye. These women often perished during childbirth or lost their babies. *Author's collection*.

SITE OF
BERACHAH HOME AND CEMETERY

THE BERACHAH RESCUE SOCIETY WAS
ORGANIZED AT WACO IN 1894 BY THE
REV. J. T. UPCHURCH (b. 1870) FOR THE
PROTECTION OF HOMELESS GIRLS AND
UNWED MOTHERS. NINE YEARS LATER
HE OPENED THE BERACHAH INDUSTRIAL
HOME AT THIS SITE. TEN BUILDINGS
WERE LOCATED HERE, INCLUDING A
PRINT SHOP FOR PUBLICATION OF THE
"PURITY JOURNAL". THE CEMETERY,
WHICH CONTAINS MORE THAN EIGHTY
GRAVES, WAS FIRST USED IN 1904 FOR
THE BURIAL OF EUNICE WILLIAMS, ONE
OF THE RESIDENTS. THE HOME CLOSED
IN 1935, BUT THE SITE WAS USED
UNTIL 1942 AS AN ORPHANAGE RUN
BY UPCHURCH'S DAUGHTER ALLIE MAE
AND HER HUSBAND FRANK WIESE.
(1981)

The cemetery lays hidden in the middle of Doug Russell Park. *Michael Barera.*

The building was transformed into an orphanage in 1935, when the Upchurch family passed the business down to their daughter. In the late 1960s, the daughter demolished the building, but the cemetery remained. Visitors rediscovered the graveyard in 1981.

Due to the elevated risk factors in giving birth in the late 1800s and early 1900s, many women and their unborn babies lost their lives. At times, a doctor could save only one life. Many of the burials at this cemetery are of stillborn babies. Gravestones are marked "twins" or "baby" or have simply a first name. The practice of generic tombstones protected the unwed mother's identity, and many babies were too young to receive a name.

Those visiting the cemetery report a feeling of being watched. Shadowy figures dart in and out from the surrounding trees. Some visitors hear laughing or talking. The sensation of a small hand touching an arm or tugging hair is not uncommon. Toys appear and disappear, indicating children playing among the tombstones.

Bethel Cemetery (Dallas County)

In 1853, the Bethel Cemetery opened. It began as a private cemetery used by the landowners, but in the 1870s, they allowed others to utilize the graveyard for burial. After this, it became a public location.

Although the city of Coppell was not officially established until 1955, the first settlers arrived in the 1860s.

The cemetery was the subject of one of the most significant controversies in the town's history during the 1960s and 1970s as development reached the area. The initial plan included building the city around the cemetery plots. But Pete Wilson, secretary of the historical society, reported that in fact construction of homes on top of burials happened frequently. The developer did not realize that this was the case until after the project was complete. During an archaeological study, historians found graves spread throughout the area. Along with the possibility of homes desecrating the graves, another legend haunts the Bethel Cemetery.

The grave of Oda Kirby stumped photographers for many years. Oda was born and died on September 17, 1909. This indicates that she died at birth. Those who attempt to take photos of her tombstone find overdeveloped photos filled with orbs. At one point, Oda's gravestone shattered into several large pieces. Each piece showed orbs in the pictures.

There is also a story of five men and a boy lynched and buried at the Bethel Cemetery in 1869. Perhaps worse, rumor has it that the corpse of one evil and demented Satan worshiper was laid to rest at Bethel and brings terror despite his death.

Oda's tombstone is in a poor state, a result of frequent breaking. *Author's collection.*

BUCKNER CEMETERY (COLLIN COUNTY)

John and Polly McGarrah came with their family and settled in the Buckner area in 1842. They were the third settlers in the area, and they opened a trading post to help draw others to the site. Construction proved challenging, as the Natives were hostile and did not welcome the new intruders on their land. Fort Buckner developed thanks to the trading post initiated by the McGarrahs. The city center brought visitors every third Monday for public executions, and these gatherings were a time for families to have picnics. Farmers and artisans set up small stalls to sell their goods.

The Texas legislature selected Buckner as the county seat for Collin County in April 1846, and three months later, an official election provided the proper officials. In November of the same year, the post office opened in Buckner, and John McGarrah became the postmaster. The town of Buckner thrived. But there was one problem. The actual town of Buckner sat three miles outside of the radius for the county seat. When legislators reevaluated this matter, they selected McKinney as the county seat. Collin County was the nearest settlement to the area and one of the signers of the

Kiowa chief Spotted Tail dug day and night to help bury those who succumbed to smallpox. His help was greatly appreciated but resulted in him contracting the disease and dying soon after. *Library of Congress*.

Texas Declaration of Independence. Settlers chose to move due to the well-established area and the county seat, and they went to live and conduct their business away from Buckner.

Today, not much remains of Buckner—a few houses, businesses and the old cemetery. The historic cemetery is unmaintained and located in the middle of a parking lot for the local flea market. The cemetery inhabitants include many of the early settlers of Collin County. In 1870, an epidemic of smallpox took the lives of many residents. One of the smallpox victims was Chief Spotted Tail, a member of the Kiowa tribe who perished from the virus in 1873. His grave is unmarked, despite the fact that he brought over two hundred tribe members to Buckner in the 1840s and was known as a hero. The chief and his tribe protected the city from hostiles.

The cemetery faced neglect. Trespassers knocked over grave markers and vandalized the majority of the cemetery. This desecration of graves might contribute to the hauntings on the small plot of land.

Many believe that Chief Spotted Tail haunts or lingers around at the Buckner Cemetery. The chief watched over the people in the nearby towns during his life and has continued to keep a watchful and protective eye on the people who come to visit Buckner Cemetery. One witness reported seeing the ghost of the chief leaning against a tree. By the time she got the attention of those with her, the chief had disappeared. Visitors attending the flea market report the feeling of being watched.

MILLS CEMETERY, THE GRAVE OF MR. SMILEY (DALLAS COUNTY)

Edward Mills established Mills Cemetery in 1854 when his wife, Elizabeth, passed away. The cemetery holds well over two thousand graves, many of which belong to the tornado victims of 1927.

North Texas is no stranger to storms, and tornados have their season. In the early morning hours of May 9, 1927, a violent thunderstorm woke the residents of Dallas County. Dark and dreary clouds appeared, and a near-constant flash of lightning illuminated the sky as the thunder roared. A fierce tornado touched down near the area now known as Garland. It momentarily lifted but then dropped back down to resume its reign of terror on the land.

The tornado left behind property damage estimated at almost $75,000. Even by today's standards, the financial loss was great. And in 1927, it was

The eeriest factor of the Smiley tombstone is the ominous death date of the entire family. Newspaper articles detail the tragic natural disaster that struck the area. Brownsville Herald.

catastrophic. The tornado destroyed twelve homes and several downtown businesses and killed seventeen people. The deaths included the mayor, Stephen Nicholson, and his mother, Missouri Nicholson.

One family lost more members than any other in town and almost lost the accurate account of their deaths as a result of urban legends. Visitors to Mills Cemetery will find one tombstone indicating the death of five family members on the same day. The marker includes thirty-seven-year-old Charles Smiley; his thirty-six-year-old wife, Belle; and their daughters Lilith, twelve; Greta, eleven; and Charlena, one. Multiple family members dying on the same day was not unheard of in the late 1920s, as disease often spread quickly in families, and medicine was far less advanced. Rumors began when cemetery visitors attempted to learn the fate of the Smiley family without researching their demise through proper channels.

The urban legend states that it would be nearly impossible for a visitor to sit back up if they lay down on the Smiley grave at midnight. The lore says that it would feel as if someone was wrapping their arms around the visitor and holding them to the ground in an effort to add one more body to the grave.

The question remained: Why? The Smiley name itself is unusual, and five family members dying on the same day is odd. It did not take long for storytellers to create a storyline fit for a horror movie. Charles Smiley became a dark, mysterious and creepy villain. He was so dark that, one night around midnight, he slipped into a fit of rage. Unable to control his actions, Smiley violently killed his wife and three daughters. As his anger subsided, he looked around the room to see a bloody mess and the four lifeless bodies of his dear family members. Unable to live with his actions, he slipped a noose around his neck and hanged himself. This mean and angry man continues to haunt the site of his family's burial and those who visit it. Visitors to the cemetery at night report footsteps on the leaves when no one is around. They also report the sound of moaning and seeing strange lights. Charles Smiley makes all the ghostly actions.

It is possible that Charles Smiley haunts the Mills Cemetery, but not for the reasons stated in the urban legend. For Charles, his wife and three daughters died as victims of the deadly tornado. Newspaper accounts report that the Smiley family suffered from the most significant loss of life on that dark Sunday morning. The family started with seven members, and only two survived the path of the fatal storm. Dorit, seven, and her sister Margaret, four, were rescued and taken to the local hospital. Officials believed that Margaret would not live through the night, but against all odds, she did.

IOOF CEMETERY (DENTON COUNTY)

The Independent Order of Odd Fellows began in London, England, in 1748 and came to America via Baltimore, Maryland, in 1819. It would take approximately twenty years for it to reach Texas and even longer to reach Denton, in 1859. Men joined as "Odd Fellows"; women joined as "Rebekahs." Their motto is "Friendship, love, and truth." Many famous men have belonged to the IOOF, including Ulysses S. Grant and Franklin D. Roosevelt.

James Smoot donated a plot of land for a cemetery for members and family members of the IOOF. The land served as the main cemetery in Denton in the early 1880s, and when land became scarce, the organization

The International Order of Odd Fellows Cemetery is often referred to as IOOF Cemetery. *Author's collection.*

The IOOF Cemetery holds over seven thousand graves. Many belong to prominent residents of the city. *Author's collection.*

added more land. In 1860, the first burial in the cemetery was for Anna Carroll, the infant daughter of Joseph and Celia Carroll. Denton's prominent men and women and city founders belonged to the IOOF and, at their deaths, resided in this cemetery.

In 1933, the deed to the cemetery went to Denton for inclusion in the parks and recreation department. The cemetery, nestled just five blocks from the historic Denton Square and courthouse, has over seven thousand graves.

Several ghost stories accompany the history of the IOOF Cemetery. Visitors often report hearing an infant crying. The infant might be Anna Carroll, reminding folks that she was the first to arrive and will be the last

The wings of the angel on Minnie Anderson's tombstone are said to move on their own. *Author's collection.*

The infant daughter of Charles and Minnie Anderson was laid to rest with her mother. *Author's collection.*

to leave. Or it could be one of the numerous infants buried in this area. Death often came quickly in the 1800s for newborns and, sometimes, their mothers.

John Anderson and his son Charles opened a private bank in Ardmore, Oklahoma. Two years after opening, the bank received a national charter grant. It was the first charted bank in Indigenous territory. With his professional life set, Charles and his wife, Minnie, began to have a family. On December 16, 1891, Minnie delivered a stillborn baby. Minnie and her family originated from Denton, Texas, and it seemed fitting to place a memorial for the infant at the IOOF Cemetery. Just four days after mourning the loss of their child, Charles faced another death: his wife, Minnie. Erected at the IOOF Cemetery is a beautiful statue of an angel overlooking the small grave marker for the infant. It is as if Minnie is there to look over her child, even in death. Those who have lived in Denton long enough will tell a tale of the angel in the cemetery. Numerous visitors claim to see the wings of the angel move, despite their stone configuration.

In 1881, Sam Bayless arrived in Denton with his wife, Elizabeth. Bayless ran a landscaping business and nursery, which was profitable enough for Sam and Elizabeth to construct a beautiful, Victorian-style home for their family. Bayless employed local workers to assist with his business. In November 1919, he found himself in a heated argument with one of his workers over financial matters. The dispute escalated from verbal threats to a fistfight. Bayless ran to his home and retrieved a shotgun, according to court documents. When he walked past his wife, she noted excessive blood staining his white shirt and learned of her husband's stabbing during the altercation. Concerned over his well-being, she prevented him from exiting the home and tended to his profuse bleeding. Bayless died in his home before the town doctor could arrive. Buried at the IOOF Cemetery, Bayless might still roam the city. Ghost stories regarding the Bayless home are abundant, and many people believe he strolls through the cemetery. Perhaps Sam Bayless checks to ensure that the landscapers are keeping the lawn mown and weeds cleared.

10

APPARITION ATTRACTIONS

Haunted attractions are not new. They have entertained people since the early nineteenth century. One of the first well-known attractions, the Chamber of Horrors, exhibited creations from the world-renowned queen of wax sculptures, Marie Tussaud, and opened its doors in 1802 in London, England. The chamber nestled in the basement of the London Planetarium attracted people like bees to honey.

The exhibit featured notorious murderers, decapitated casualties, infamous historical figures like Marie Antoinette and King Louis XVI and grotesque death masks from several victims of the guillotine. Many of the featured sculptures came from the collection of Dr. Philippe Curtis, who had displayed his waxworks in Paris in 1782. This Swiss physician was the wax modeler who taught Tussaud to create lifelike sculptures. He left his entire collection to Tussaud when he passed away in 1794. This haunting attraction brought visitors and money, but the unanswered question remained: Why?

The answer is simple. When fear presents itself, the human body shifts into fight-or-flight mode. During this stage, the body releases adrenaline, endorphins and dopamine. Together, these biochemicals create a rush, giving a sense of euphoria if the chemicals are in a controlled environment, like an artificial haunted house.

Contemporary haunted attractions come to life with actors, theatrics, robotics, sound effects and pyrotechnics. They cater to recognized fears, such as claustrophobia (enclosed spaces), ophidiophobia (snakes), arachnophobia (spiders), thanatophobia (death), xenophobia (unknown) and phasmophobia (ghosts). A detailed backstory is key to the success of a ghostly attraction. Backstories come from the history of the location, the inventive mind of the creator or true stories. While guests find themselves led down twisty paths with lots of turns, the lights are dim or nonexistent. Stimulation of the senses begins with loud noises and strobe lights, which temporarily distract the mind from the jump scare of a creepy clown, chainsaw-wielding maniac or brain-seeking zombie. If one of the haunted locations in the previous chapters did not send a chill down your spine, here is a list of a few noteworthy haunted manufactured attractions scattered throughout North Texas.

HAUNTED SHADOWS LAKE TRAIL (DENTON COUNTY)

The Haunted Shadows Lake Trail (www.hauntedshadowslaketrail.com) opened in 2010 and encompasses a trail just over one mile long for visitors to hike and seek adventure.

The storyline of this attraction is convincing and sounds like tales that have come down through the years. Years ago, a local farmer, Jeremiah Brody, one of the "good ol' boys," found a unique way to profit from misfortune. He accepted troubled youths to work on his secluded farmland for a reasonable fee. Local law enforcement supported the idea and felt it was a great way to help steer troublemakers onto the correct path in life. After all, asylums worked well in the past to hide these embarrassing "situations" from society, but few remained open. Local jails and juvenile detention centers lacked funding and struggled with overcrowding. Brody offered to make these problems "go away."

As time passed, Brody's farm gained many workers. The circus dropped off its runaways and freak-show youths as it passed by the farm. Brody gained free farmworkers, and he was smart enough to charge a fee to care for the troubled youths.

His out-of-sight and out-of-mind system provided a way for these troubled souls to seek a prosecution-free environment and lifestyle. The youths paid a hefty price to avoid jail. They found themselves isolated and rejected by society. They worked long hours on the farm and almost died there. Their final resting place included a makeshift cemetery in an unmarked and sometimes multi-bodied grave. Brody's reign of terror did not end until he passed away. Now the souls of these forgotten youths remain on the land, eager to haunt visitors with their hatred for society.

HATCH AND KRAVEN'S SLAUGHTERHOUSE (GRAYSON COUNTY)

Hatch and Kraven's Slaughterhouse (www.hatchandkravens.com) is considered one of the scariest haunts in North Texas. One reviewer called it "your worst nightmare!"

The legend of Hatch and Kraven started in 1930, when famine, poverty and despair filled the days. The small town of Sherman, Texas, was not immune to the Depression, and the residents struggled to keep alive.

Hatch Modair and his brother Kraven grew up raised by their father, a butcher by trade. The boys spent most of their time alongside their father in the slaughterhouse and quickly learned the trade. Kraven was just twenty-one when his father died from the plague, and his mother became extremely ill. He became responsible for his sixteen-year-old brother and the slaughterhouse's day-to-day business.

Cattle, which frequently moved through Texas in large cattle drives, became scarce as the economy crashed. Slaughterhouses required cattle to survive. Kraven knew he needed to find a way to keep the money flowing, as his brother's welfare was in his hands. Hatch stayed home to care for their ailing mother, and Kraven went to the slaughterhouse every day.

One day, Kraven came face-to-face with an angry customer asking for meat. The slaughterhouse had few cows, and the meat stocks were at an all-time low. The disgruntled customer lashed out at Kraven, and a fight ensued. Workers attempted to stop the fight, but it was too late. The customer was dead, and Kraven had a huge problem.

The workers dragged the body to the back and did what butchers do best. They chopped the body into small pieces and processed each part as they had done so many times before with cattle. They stocked the freezer with the body parts. It appeared that a new source of meat had arrived in the slaughterhouse.

As time passed and cattle continued to be scarce, the butchers found lost travelers and runaways. They sought victims whom society already deemed invisible. They continued to keep a complete meat source to feed the community.

Thrillvania Haunted House Park (Kaufman County)

Ranked one of the top five "cannot miss haunted attractions" in 2021, Thrillvania Haunted House Park (www.thrillvania.com) is not the average haunted house. It is a stately manor with a dark, dark past.

The legend begins in 1901, when builders constructed a manor on over fifty acres of land. The neighbors kept to themselves, as the new structure sat nestled next to an old plantation cemetery. The Verdun Manor was home to Baron Michael Verdun. He was not your average baron. During episodes of the full moon, he grew hair and claws and transformed into a werewolf. His lovely wife, Cassandra D'Arque, had a thirst for blood and frequently turned into a bat. The couple was eccentric, to say the least. Nevertheless, the antebellum-style manor was perfect for a mad scientist and his wife to create a life together.

Cassandra lured wayward travelers onto the manor grounds at night with her beauty and grace. The baron brought in foreign workers to dig deep into the cellar floors. He also had them dig up bodies from the cemetery to extend his property line. Surely no one would miss a body or two. These innocent victims became the subject of Verdun's crazy experiments, which included cruel and painful procedures. The victims, if they lived, found themselves severely deformed and hideous. They were no longer men and yet not quite beasts.

The scientist's completed project was not known, but the land surrounding his home became flooded with the failed products of his experiments. These creatures left the manor, free to fend for themselves, and they often would not or could not travel far from the manor. They acted as guard dogs, keeping unwanted visitors away.

The townsfolk became informed and grew curious. They formed a plan to keep the town safe from the creatures. They would capture and kill the baron and his wife. Cassandra was trapped in her crypt. There she was decapitated and mutilated. The baron was also captured and faced brutal bludgeoning before being repeatedly stabbed until the life force left his body. The two were buried together in a shallow grave in front of the manor. This grave served as a reminder of the terror the town had faced.

One year later, Vincent Carruthers purchased the manor. The real estate agent had been dishonest with him and did not disclose the manor's ominous history. One Halloween night, the Carruthers family hosted a gala. The Verdun couple did not appreciate the gala held in "their" manor without them. So they dug their way out of the cold, shallow grave and joined the party. They then brutally murdered the Carruthers family and all of the guests. It seemed fitting to place the corpses throughout the estate's grounds in a grotesque gesture to warn visitors or potential buyers of their fate.

Resuming ownership of the manor, the Verduns also resumed their risky experiments.

Reindeer Manor (Ellis County)

"This is going on our forty-third season. We are the oldest haunted house in Texas, and we have not found evidence of any haunt in the country that's older than this one," said Alex Lohmann more than five years ago.

This means that the attraction is nearing fifty seasons at the time of this writing.

The oldest haunted attraction in the state is remarkable, but age is not the only feature that sets Reindeer Manor apart from other local haunts. Not every spooky attraction can say that it stands on a haunted location with a shady history. The owner and operators at Reindeer Manor will neither confirm nor deny that ghosts haunt their location. They will, however, tell the haunting tale of the manor's history. Documents have proved difficult to recover, as the story begins in the early 1900s.

"This house was built after the wood frame house here burned down in 1910," explained Alex Lohman of Reindeer Manor.

James Sharp rented his home to a farmer and his family. The renter killed his entire family in the home before taking his own life. In light of the tragic event, Sharp decided to rebuild but chose the ground where a smaller home had burned to the ground. The records again are not clear, but newspaper articles report that Sharp died from a gunshot wound to the head, and most believe he took his own life prior to the completion of the new home. It is uncertain who fired the fatal shot. Stories tell of Sharp being involved in an affair, which his wife then discovered.

The coroner reported on "the loss of two to three ounces of brain substance."

Just when the story seemed that it could not possibly get worse, it did.

In 1920, Sharp's son Matt took over construction of the new home. He developed the property by adding several buildings and farming the land. Despite his father's death, the location took a turn for the better, and by all accounts the family had a successful ranch and manor. But the

Great Depression struck in 1929, and in its path of destruction, the Sharp family fell.

The manor staff distanced themselves from the negativity by avoiding contact with the Sharp family. Mrs. Sharp was a spiritualist and believed the family was suffering under an unbreakable curse. As money disappeared, so did Matt's sanity.

Set on finding a cure for their situation, the Sharps sought help and advice from anyone who listened. They called in witch doctors, spiritualists and psychics and invited their staff to join in on chanting incantations believed to help ease the wicked curse. Mrs. Sharp led séances to call to the spirits on the other side and ask for advice.

In the end, the answer they so desperately sought appeared before their eyes. In order to end the Sharp family curse, they needed to end the family line. When Matt discovered his wife's lifeless body and a bottle of poison tonic, he grabbed a rope and headed to the barn. When officials later discovered the couple, Mrs. Sharp lay dead from poison and Matt was swinging from the rafters of the old barn with a noose around his neck. The Sharp family line ended. It seemed that tragedy had free rein in the structure around the current attraction's lands.

The electricity in the building goes off and on without anyone doing so. Sometimes, the owners find the light switches changed but no living person nearby. The owners note that they hear footsteps and loud arguments when no one is around. One night, the owners' son reported seeing a ghostly shadow figure of a man walking into the barn where Matt Sharp hanged himself.

When asked to describe the man, Lohmann's son said, "Oh, dad…the man did not have a face."

The true history of the location involves hauntings, but the attraction is also vamped up with Halloween theatrics. The Reindeer Manor truly comes to life after dark.

THE PARKER HOUSE (DENTON COUNTY)

The Parker Funeral Home was a local operation, and the family ran Denton, Texas. Young Mary Parker played and lived among the dead for many years while her parents operated the funeral home. Constant exposure to funerals from an early age caused Mary to become desensitized to human life and death.

Around 1940, Mr. and Mrs. Parker met their end in a fatal airplane crash. Mary swiftly took over the family business. As larger, corporate mortuaries entered the industry, small family mortuaries suffered. The Parker business slowed, and the money disappeared quickly. Mary needed to develop a business idea to keep the family firm afloat.

She found a cure for her financial woes, but she needed to keep things under wraps. When a family dropped their loved one off for cremation or mortuary services, Mary harvested all viable organs and sold them to various buyers at a profitable value. The family members did not question what they could not see, and Mary soon had more money than she could spend. That did not stop her from continuing to harvest organs and profit from it. She extracted from the victims brought to her mortuary until she found that her buyers' demands exceeded her supply. As time passed, her heart grew colder. She preyed on the homeless and runaways. She led them into her trap and, using her live victims, found ways to harvest organs via torture and despair.

One day, a transient man fell prey to Mary but managed to escape with his life and went to the police. The victim's testimony prompted an investigation and the eventual seizure of the home. The home remained in official custody for about twenty years as investigators attempted to piece together what exactly happened there. The current owner purchased the home and restored it to its previous state.

The home was cleared out and turned into a haunted attraction featuring four different haunts—five, including the manor's history.

Theta Omega Kappa throws a Halloween party at the legendary Reindeer Manor; this is the site's first attraction. Unknown to partygoers, a "serial killer" escaped the psych ward and roams the manor. The Copycat Killer wears a cat mask as he stalks and slashes his way through the party. Like any other frat party, there are plenty of alcoholic beverages and distracted young adults.

The 13th Street Morgue storyline goes back to the original owner of the land and allegedly began operations when Jonathon Maybrick leased one of the barns on the manor's property for his residence and funeral parlor. Maybrick's funeral home did well after performing a service for a notorious criminal, Raymond Reynolds. During a bank robbery, Reynolds shot and killed a bank teller and a sixteen-year-old bank patron named Abigail Helm. Police stopped Reynolds with a fatal bullet before he could escape.

Abigail's father was devastated when he heard that the murderer of his innocent daughter was to have a proper funeral service. It was close to Christmas, so Maybrick decided to postpone the funeral to avoid a confrontation with Mr. Helm.

Helm broke into the funeral home on December 13 dressed as Santa Claus in order to trick the Maybrick children in the event that they woke up. He then strangled Maybrick and his wife before shooting himself in the chest in the parlor of the funeral home.

The barn housing the funeral parlor was the same barn where Matt Sharp hanged himself from the rafters.

The video game machine for Dungeons of Doom sits by itself in the corner of a dark, abandoned arcade. Once the most popular game in the arcade, its popularity fell, and players moved on to other pursuits of victory. And this brings us to the next attraction.

In 1987, Elliot Wynn, a boy who frequented the 1-Up Arcade, spent his free time dropping quarters in the slots of video games instead of being at home. He was the typical gamer nerd who enjoyed soda and Pop Rocks while wasting his quarters on the machines. When he grew bored of the popular games, he wandered around the arcade, searching for something that might catch his attention. Then he discovered an old, dust-covered game in the back: Dungeons of Doom.

He dropped a quarter in the machine, and much to his surprise, the game came to life with bright lights and a retro music track. Elliot played for thirteen hours before he defeated the game. But before he could enjoy his victory, the machine cracked open and sucked Elliot's body into a vortex. He realized his mistake and his new fate, but Elliot is trapped in the Dungeons of Doom machine until the next player comes along and defeats the high score.

The final haunt brings involves B.E.S.E.R.K. Industries, an elite military unit that has discovered a breakthrough in a formerly abandoned intercontinental ballistic missile program. This breakthrough led to the discovery of unidentified aircraft and alien technology. It is up to B.E.S.E.R.K. to fight a powerful, enhanced humanoid force affected by a drug known as "Project RM47." The visitors to this haunt are survivors of the biochemical outbreak and are escorted through the bunker by the particular military unit. The mutated scientists and flesh-eating creatures from failed lab experiments chase the survivors.

THE HAUNTED ATTRACTIONS IN North Texas are as grand and big as the state itself. There are too many to mention in this short chapter, but a quick Google search can point visitors in the right direction.

Everything in Texas is bigger and better, whether it is genuine ghosts haunting old sites or manufactured attractions bringing visitors from all over the state. Thrill-seekers in North Central Texas will not be disappointed.

WORKS CITED

Adolphus Hotel. https://www.adolphus.com/history.

Arnold, Ann. *Gamblers & Gangsters: Fort Worth's Jacksboro Highway in the 1940s & 1950s.* Woodway, TX: Eakin Press, 1998.

Baker Hotel. "History." Accessed December 12, 2019. https://thebakerhotelandspa.com.

Baker, Terry. *Hangings and Lynchings in Dallas County, Texas, 1853 to 1920.* Woodway, TX: Eakin Press, 2016.

Brown, Alan, and Heather Adel Wiggins. *Haunted Texas: Ghosts and Strange Phenomena of the Lone Star State.* Mechanicsburg, PA: Stackpole Books, 2008.

Burleson's Honey. http://www.burlesons-honey.com.

Caddo Nation. https://mycaddonation.com.

Carter, Cecile Elkins. *Caddo Indians: Where We Come From.* Norman: University of Oklahoma Press, 1995.

Cartwright, Gary. "Showdown at Waggoner Ranch." *Texas Monthly*, January 1, 2004. https://www.texasmonthly.com.

Clendenin, Mary Joe, and Joe Fitzgerald. *The Ghost of the Mcdow Hole.* Lubbock, TX: Clendenin Enterprises, 1991.

Collin County History. https://www.collincountyhistory.com.

Colony (TX) Courier-Leader. "Denton County Event Honors Officers Killed in the Line of Duty." May 14, 2008. https://starlocalmedia.com/thecolonycourierleader.

Cook, Rita. *Haunted Dallas.* Charleston, SC: The History Press, 2011.

———. *Haunted Fort Worth.* Charleston, SC: The History Press, 2011.

Cox, John. "Houdini's Favorite Hotel Seeking Redevelopment." *Wild About Harry* (blog), January 27, 2017. https://www.wildabouthoudini.com.

Crumpton, Taylor. "111 Years after His Death, Dallas Acknowledges the Lynching of Allen Brooks in Downtown." Dallas Historical Society. "Hangings and Lynchings in Dallas County, Texas 1853–1920 (2017-04-11)." http://www.dallashistory.org.

Dallas Terrors. "The Haunted Adolphus Hotel." Accessed November 6, 2021. https://dallasterrors.com.

Decatur Town Square. "Ghosts on Decatur Town Square?" October 23, 2016. https://www.decaturtownsquare.com.

Denton History. "Building the Denton County Courthouse: 1895–1897." http://dentonhistory.net.

D Magazine, February 22, 2022. https://www.dmagazine.com.

———. "Royally Haunted: The Adolphus Hotel." February 23, 2021, https://www.dmagazine.com.

Dillard, Coshandra. "In Downtown Dallas, a Crowd of 5,000 Watched This Black Man Get Lynched—and They Took Souvenirs." Timeline, October 16, 2017. https://timeline.com.

Encyclopædia Britannica. "Caddo." https://www.britannica.com.

Enlow, Jeremy. *Cowboys of the Waggoner Ranch*. N.p.: Jeremy Enlow Fine Art Photography, 2015.

Fahy, Claire. "Allen Brooks, Victim of a 1910 Lynching, Is Remembered in Dallas." *New York Times*, November 20, 2021.

Fisher, Dawn. "Haunting of Mcdow Hole on Highway 6." Texas Hill Country, July 29, 2016. https://texashillcountry.com.

Ford, Ashley. "Rogers Hotel Resident Recalls Unexplainable Events in 'Haunted' Building." *Waxahachie (TX) Daily Light*, October 30, 2018.

Gilbreath, West C. *Death on the Gallows: The Encyclopedia of Legal Hangings in Texas*. Fort Worth, TX: Wild Horse Press, 2017.

Gosbee, Donna. "Jane Elkins—A Female Slave, Jane Elkins, Becomes the First Woman to Be Legally Executed in the State of Texas When She Is Hung on Friday, May 27, 1853 beside the Dallas County Courthouse." Human Rights Dallas Maps. http://www.humanrightsdallasmaps.com.

Hatch & Kraven's Slaughterhouse. Accessed September 10, 2021. http://hatchandkravens.com.

Haunted Rooms America. "The Most Haunted Places in Dallas–Fort Worth, TX." Accessed December 16, 2021. https://www.hauntedrooms.com.

Haunted Shadows Lake Trail. http://hauntedshadowslaketrail.com.

Heid, Jason. "Ghosts of Dallas: Old Red Courthouse, 1963." *D Magazine*, October 22, 2014. https://www.dmagazine.com.

Lake Texoma. "History." https://www.laketexoma.com.

Landau, Mia Sherwood. "Four Ghost Towns under Lake Texoma." Lake Texoma. https://www.laketexoma.com.

Lang, George. "Uncovering Lake Texoma's Submerged Ghost Towns." *405 Magazine*, February 10, 2022. https://www.405magazine.com.

Lankford, George E. *Native American Legends: Southeastern Legends—Tales from the Natchez, Caddo, Biloxi, Chickasaw, and Other Nations.* Atlanta, GA: August House, 1987.

Lantz, Gene. "Jane Elkins Died for Us." *Gene Lantz* (blog), June 6, 2016. https://genelantz.org.

Library of Congress. Chronicling America. "All Digitized Newspapers." https://chroniclingamerica.loc.gov/newspapers/.

———. "The Waxahachie Daily Light. [Volume] (Waxahachie, Tex.) 1894–Current, November 18, 1911, Image 1." https://chroniclingamerica.loc.gov.

Livingston, Ronald Howard. "The Ghosts at Thistle Hill." Historical Ghost Stories of Texas. October 24, 2016. http://ghoststories.brazoriaresearch.com.

M.E. Grenander Department of Special Collections & Archives. "Documentation for the Execution of Stephen Ballew." May 24, 1872. https://archives.albany.edu.

Moonlit Road. "Southern Ghost Stories, Folktales, Storytelling." Accessed May 1, 2020. https://www.themoonlitroad.com.

Murphy, S. Holland, et al. "A Gruesome Timeline of the Adolphus Hotel's Potential Ghosts." *D Magazine*, October 12, 2018. https://www.dmagazine.com.

Nacogdoches History & Culture. "Caddo Indians of Texas." https://www.visitnacogdoches.org.

Newberry, Barbara Y., and David W. Aiken. *Weatherford, Texas.* Charleston, SC: Arcadia Press, 1999.

NTParanormal. Accessed September 17, 2020. https://www.ntparanormal.com.

Officer Down Memorial Page. "Jailer Floyd Coberly." Accessed February 23, 2022. https://www.odmp.org.

Old Red Museum of Dallas County History & Culture. https://www.oldred.org.

Owens, Marjorie, and Jordan Armstrong.. "31 North Texas Hauntings." WFAA, October 27, 2016, https://www.wfaa.com.

Parker House. "Haunted House: Denton, Texas." https://www.hauntedhousedenton.com.

Pate, J'Nell L. *Fort Worth Stockyards*. Charleston, SC: Arcadia Press, 2009.

Portal to Texas History. "The Daily Courier-Gazette (Mckinney, Tex.), Vol. 26, Ed. 1 Friday, November 17, 1922." Accessed March 27, 2020. https://texashistory.unt.edu.

Porter, Roze McCoy. *Thistle Hill: The Cattle Baron's Legacy*. Dallas, TX: Taylor Publishing, 1980.

Reindeer Manor Halloween Park. http://www.reindeermanor.com.

Rich, Harold. *Fort Worth: Outpost, Cowtown, Boomtown*. Norman: University of Oklahoma Press, 2014.

Roberts, Kim. "Dallas County's 'Old Red' Courthouse Undergoing Evaluation for Use as Appellate Court." The Texan. January 28, 2020, https://staging.thetexan.news.

Roberts, Tim. "DFW Ghost Stories: Haunted History a Permanent Guest at Rogers Hotel." KDAF The CW33, October 31, 2015. https://cw33.com.

Smith, Foster Todd. *The Caddo Indians: Tribes at the Convergence of Empires, 1542–1854*. College Station: Texas A&M University Press, 1995.

Strange State. "Zoo Keeper Works Overtime—From beyond the Grave." April 2, 2013. https://strangestate.blogspot.com.

Texas Genealogy Trails. "Murder of Hardy Mills of Collin County, Texas." https://genealogytrails.com/tex.

Texas Historical Commission. "Denton County Courthouse—Denton." https://www.thc.texas.gov.

Texas State Historical Association. "H. Allen Anderson." https://www.tshaonline.org.

———. "Lake Texoma." https://www.tshaonline.org.

———. "Thistle Hill." https://www.tshaonline.org.

———. "Wise County." https://www.tshaonline.org.

TexPartParanormalLLC. "Investigations." https://www.texpartparanormal.com.

Thrillvania Haunted House Park. Accessed February 7, 2022. https://thrillvania.com.

Treat, Shaun. "Denton's Most Haunted Places." Denton Convention & Visitors Bureau, September 7, 2022. https://www.discoverdenton.com.

UNT Libraries' Digital Projects. "The Portal to Texas History." https://texashistory.unt.edu.

U.S. Army Corps of Engineers. Tulsa District. "History of Lake Texoma." https://www.swt.usace.army.mil.

Whitington, Mitchel. *Ghosts of North Texas*. Lanham, MD: Republic of Texas Press, 2004.

Wise County Historical Society. http://www.wisehistory.com.

W.T. Waggoner Ranch. https://waggonerranch.com.

Youngblood, Dawn. *Fort Worth*. Charleston, SC: Arcadia Press, 2019.

About the Author

Teresa Nordheim is an award-winning author with more than fifty published articles and four books to her credit. Having made her home in Texas, she loves exploring its landscapes by researching its mysteries. Check out her other books: *Haunted Tacoma*, *Wicked Seattle* and *Murder and Mayhem in Seattle*.